SAVING THE JEWISH FAMILY

Myths and Realities in the Diaspora
Strategies for the Future
An Analysis and Cumulative Bibliography
1970-1982

Gerald B. Bubis

UNIVERSITY
PRESS OF
AMERICA

Lanham • New York • London

THE JERUSALEM CENTER FOR
PUBLIC AFFAIRS/
CENTER FOR JEWISH
COMMUNITY STUDIES

British Cataloging in Publication Information Available

Co-published by arrangement with The Jerusalem Center
for Public Affairs/Center for Jewish Community Studies

ISBN: 0-8191-6575-1 (pbk. : alk. paper)
ISBN: 0-8191-6574-3 (alk. paper)

All University Press of America books are produced on acid-free
paper which exceeds the minimum standards set by the National
Historical Publication and Records Commission.

ACKNOWLEDGMENTS

The support and encouragement of many colleagues have added to my learning. I thank especially Professor Daniel Elazar at the Jerusalem Center for Public Affairs who has helped in ways beyond measure. Professor U. O. Schmetz and Dr. S. Della Pergola were kind enough to share unpublished data.

My former student, Harriet Kaplowitz, worked diligently as my research assistant. The staff and editors at the Jerusalem Center were of inestimable help as has always been the case over the years.

My colleagues at Hebrew Union College have critiqued my work and broadened my horizons. Certainly the same must be said of Professors Alfred Gottschalk and Uri Herscher, President and Vice President of Hebrew Union College, who have encouraged me in my work.

Lastly, thanks to my wife, Ruby, chaver im leben who has been my mentor and helpmeet for nearly four decades.

All errors and omissions are mine.

Gerald B. Bubis
Jerusalem 1985

TABLE OF CONTENTS

LIST OF TABLES   Page   vii

PREFACE   ix

INTRODUCTION - Life is Metamorphosis   xiii

I   TRENDS: Jews in the Diaspora   1

II   BACKGROUND: The Jewish Family   5
       Functions of the Family

III   DEMOGRAPHIC DATA   13

IV   THE UNITED STATES AND ISRAEL   23

V   TRENDS: An Analysis   37
       Impact on the Future
       Services Available: Implications
       Problems in Israel

VI   VALUES IN WESTERN SOCIETY   57
       Defining Values
       The American Value Base
       Ethnicity
       The Jewish Response

VII   BACKGROUND: Defining Jewish Life   65

VIII   CHALLENGES AND STRATEGIES: Working
       With Jews in the Decades Ahead   73
       Focus on the Family
       Implications for Policy and Action

IX   AN AGENDA FOR THE AMERICAN JEWISH
       COMMUNITY   81
       Conscious Choosing
       Jewish Community Institutions
       Coordination and Reordering Priorities

NOTES   91

CUMULATIVE BIBLIOGRAPHY   103

TABLES

Table I   Divorce Rate Per 1000 Marriages   Page   7

Table II   Personal Values: "New Breed Versus
               Traditional Parents"   9

Table III   World Jewish Population Estimates
               (1975)   14

Table IV   Rate of Natural Movement Among
               Jews and General Population by
               Country and Period, (per 1,000
               Population)   16-17

Table V   Jewish Marriage Rates and
               Current Frequencies of Mixed
               Marriages Among Selected Jewish
               Populations in Europe, 1958-1977   18-19

Table VI   Number of Divorces in Israel   28

Table VII   Mortality (Life Expectancy at Birth
               in Israel for Jews)   28

Table VIII   Literacy and Education Levels in
               Israel   29

Table IX   Divorce   30

Table X   Average Annual Number of
               Divorces per 1,000 Households
               With Each Number of Children
               (aged 0-17)   31

Table XI   Percentage of Respective
               Population in Israel over 55 Years
               of Age   32

Table XII   Fertility Rates Per Women in
               Israel   32

Table XIII   Rate of Participants in Civilian
               Labor Force of Jewish Women, by
               Marital Status   33

Table XIV	Years of Schooling	34
Table XV	Last School Attended	35
Table XVI	Fertility Measures of Jews and General Population by Country and Period	40-41
Table XVII	Average Number of Children Born Per Jewish Woman, by Age of Women, Country and Year	42-43
Table XVIII	Average Number of Children	44
Table XIX	Births and Deaths among Selected Jewish and General Population in Europe, 1958-1977 (Per 1,000)	45-46
Table XX	Population Over 55	47
Table XXI	Fertility Rates per Woman in Israel	47

PREFACE

This book has two objectives: to comprehend trends which are buffeting the contemporary Jewish family and to present the reactions to those trends. The main body of the book, examining and evaluating the phenomena of Jews living with post-emancipation realities, encompasses the first objective, while the extensive bibliography is a response to the second.

Trends are rarely sustained in predictable ways and, indeed, many expert futurists seem to spend as much time explaining the variable that modified their prediction as they continue to make new predictions. The reader will discover that I claim no prescience about the future even as I remain optimistic about the continuity of Jews into that future. There is as much faith in the often mysterious ways Jews have continued some corporate existence as there is evidence that their corporate creative powers have not diminished over the millennia. Certainly, a serious study of history reveals the vitality and wisdom with which Jews have continually adapted and readapted to changing environments - whether physical, psychological, theological, economic, or otherwise.

I have discussed elsewhere the notion that the majority of Jews in the world today have moved beyond being concerned only with what Towles called "common human needs" or the minimal psychic, social, and physical needs which Maslow placed at the bottom of a hierarchy. Indeed, as Elazar has pointed out in his work, the Jew has found ways to "re-covenant" each 10 generations or so, and restructure Jewish life so as to cope with the new while reaffirming and re-shaping the "truths" and Jewish traditions of old. It is my premise (1) that Jewish institutions and communities must also move beyond the minimal common denominator of helping Jews in physical and emotional distress and deal with the problems of cultural, spiritual, and emotional deprivation.

At the same time, there are real economic strains. Given the difficulties experienced by Jewish communities due to economic exigencies, there is a growing consensus about the need to strengthen Jewish lives and families through an approach which emphasizes prevention of problems, more than has been the case in the past. The first section in this book deals with the framework for these concerns.

While the bibliography has over 1,200 entries, no books are cited. Rather, I have listed only articles, believing them to be less known and less utilized by those involved in developing strategies for work with Jewish families. This listing in itself makes a powerful statement. In 1970, (2) Schlesinger provided a bibliography on the

Jewish family in his fine book. There were fewer than 400 entries. The over 1,200 articles cited here were written in North America from 1970 to 1982. Thus the amount of material devoted to the subject of the Jewish family has grown dramatically, even explosively, in the past 12 years. Heine's formulation of "as to the Christian, so the Jew" seems only partially true. In many instances, the Jew - having achieved so much in modern times - now often functions as a precursor of trends, and may be perceived as expressing social tendencies or developments before they are evident in society in general.

The classifications in the bibliography were set up to serve those interested in developing programs to save the Jewish family and thus are not geared to those whose major interest is to study the family as an evolving institution. The classifications themselves confirm the complications arising from separating myths and realities. All cultures create myths about themselves, and indeed must maintain the myths in order to sustain themselves. Jews are no different. Difficulties arise when some myths are no longer able to be sustained. Reading the categories in the bibliography which include abortion, alcoholism, divorce, mixed marriages, and the like, makes for a kind of grim shorthand description of a crumbling mythology. Many might draw the conclusion that we are not only facing the death of illusions about the Jewish family but the death of the Jewish people itself.

Nothing could be further from the truth. The basic underpinnings remain strong, and much that is good and healthy is to be found in contemporary Jewish life, even as the effects of modernity have some negative influences. Indeed, to discover that many trends seen as new are not; to ascertain that Jewish vitality is increasing and not decreasing; to confirm that most Jews still wish for and work for Jewish continuity in their homes and do not wish to disappear - all this offers much more cause for hope than despair.

Suffice it to say that the bibliography reflects the work of those who write about the disabilities, pain, and disintegration of the Jewish family. Healthy, fulfilled Jewish families do not generally "report in" to researchers, nor are their successes often dealt with in professional literature. The nature of Jewish life is such that most agencies and organizations deal with the pain of aberrant situations rather than with the normative and successful, and I have argued elsewhere about the need to demonstrate the positive realities (3) in order to retain an appropriate perspective. This is not to say that the 1,200 entries all deal with failed Jewish families; many articles also review and report on services to the well and the whole. The 69 classifications may provide a focus for reference, while the bibliography of the book itself, though not comprehensive, offers the reader access to yet other writings and research which have provided the framework for my evaluations.

It is obvious that many Jewish families are in profound trouble today and are a major focus for concern. Yet beneath the welter of articles, assessments, prescriptions, exhortations, and suggested solutions lies an important assumption: the family as an institution is needed and the growing concern and attention to it is but a reaffirmation of that fact and an expression of belief in the resiliency and abiding strength of the Jewish family in the future. This book is one more such affirmation.

The Jewish family has been discussed for millennia. Many Talmud tractates attest to its centrality in Jewish thinking; to this very day, responsa literature deals with issues of concern to the Jewish family - its definition, existence, and continuity. However, no attempt was made in the English language until relatively recently to catalog articles on the Jewish family. In the field of Jewish communal service itself, the volume Trends and Issues in Jewish Communal Service (4) highlighted some of the most representative articles in the field over a seven-decade period. Of the over 150 articles in the book, a handful were devoted to issues related to the Jewish family. Schlesinger (5) was the first to classify and annotate relevant material with 429 entries on Jewish family life worldwide. Shortly thereafter, Linzer's excellent bibliography on Jewish communal service had a few dozen entries, albeit not annotated. A representative but by no means comprehensive bibliography was published in my book Serving the Jewish Family (6). In the monumental work edited by Berger, Turbulent Decades (7), the sequel to Trends and Issues, once again a section was devoted to the Jewish family but with no attempt at bibliography.

Much remains to be done. To date, no comprehensive bibliography exists of books dealing with the Jewish family. The bibliography in this book does not include the fields of anthropology, sociology, or social psychology, but is confined primarily to social work and communal service literature. No multilingual synthesis has yet been attempted. Given the focus of this book on the trends facing Jews worldwide, there still exists a need to compile an international bibliography.

INTRODUCTION

Life is Metamorphosis

This monograph grew out of an interest of nearly two decades in exploring contemporary Jewish life. Opportunities to lecture abroad, to study and work in Israel, allowed me to examine trends in America from a broader context. This in turn intensified my thinking and concern about the issue of the future of Jews and the Jewish family. Some Jews obviously do better than others in coping with acculturation and with each other in the family. Observations in these areas of concern led me to evaluate and describe the worldwide trends as best as I could ascertain them, and to place them into an appropriate historical context. The first sections of the monograph are therefore devoted to an analysis of some historical trends and contemporary demographic data.

The last sections deal with the ethnic and value-laden realities and challenges which face each Jewish family and some of the larger issues which confront organizations and communities as they evolve strategies to strengthen those families who turn to them for guidance, values, and support.

There is much to concern us. There is even more to give us hope. My optimism emerges from the belief that being Jewish today is sustained more by will than by external accidents of history, and by my conviction that our will is alive, well, and growing.

"Life is metamorphosis. Everything else is death. There is redemption shivering and screaming out of the mouths of our young. Not a comfortable or mannerly noise, but the sound of history has never been a tinkle. To hear it might be to save ourselves." (8) Frederick Morton was responding here to the reaction of the young who first taught their elders the bitter and wounding truths about Vietnam. We who work on behalf of the Jewish people are not all young, but too often we do hear the cries of wounded people who deal with a different and much more subtle issue - the confrontation between a people's claim on its members and the larger world's enticement to abandon Jewish bonds of memory, responsibility, and behavior. In a world which sometimes seems to have gone mad, we must respond with reason - to assess reality steadfastly and then determine a course of action.

TRENDS

Jews in the Diaspora

A number of generalizations may be set forth to describe factors affecting the Jewish family worldwide outside Israel. While Israel has been affected by some of these trends, it also represents some problematic and yet-to-be-understood phenomena which may in turn have an impact on future Israel-diaspora relations. (The data from which these conclusions are drawn are cited later in this monograph.) Thus the following observations apply basically to Jews throughout the diaspora; a delineation of trends unique to Israel and the United States will be discussed in section IV.

1. Jewish families in most countries are frequently nuclear in nature; obversely, extended families are rarely the norm in any of the diaspora communities.

2. Almost all Jewish families - except for a growing but still small number of traditional families (neo-Orthodox and/or ultra-Orthodox) - have "achieved" zero population growth. Some communities have actually reached negative population growth. Until recently, however, there seemed to be a "bottom line" below which most families did not fall. As a result, the current size of Jewish families outside Israel is at a level slightly below the replacement rate needed to maintain the present population.

3. A growing number of Jews worldwide are postponing their marriages until later in life than previously. A measurable and growing minority are planning on not marrying at all. The increasing number of unmarrieds portends a further drop in future birthrates. This phenomenon, while long apparent in the general population of the West, including non-Jews as well as Jews, is relatively new for Jews of Eastern European origin.

4. Jews as an identifiable group have more elderly per thousand than their demographic neighbors - more than any other racial, ethnic, and/or religious group in the world. Put another way, the median age of Jews outside of Israel ranges from 4 to 13 years higher than the general populations in the countries in which Jews are found.

5. Divorce is increasing among Jews worldwide, and in a growing number of instances may be at an even higher rate than among non-Jews. The consequences of dealing with new "blended families,"

with "extra" sets of parents, children, and other relatives are beginning to be identified as a legitimate area for concern within families and among educational and communal service institutions.

6. There is an upward trend of mixed marriages in all diaspora communities. While this rate continues to rise in some countries, it may have stabilized in a few.

An increasing number of studies indicate that the degree of loss to the Jewish community through mixed marriage is lower than once feared. This is because a significant number of non-Jews convert to Judaism and a still greater number of mixed marrieds raise their children as Jews even when there has been no conversion. This conclusion seems sustainable even though there is evidence of a growing phenomenon of Jewish women marrying non-Jewish men, resulting in children who, while halachically Jewish by matrilineal definition, are marginal to Jewish life because they are identified sociologically as non-Jews.

7. Mobility of Jews has resulted in radical population shifts, possibly unequalled in history, accompanied by major ramifications that grow out of discontinuity. Except for the United States and Eastern Europe, there is no country in which the majority of Jews is third generation native-born, and there is but a handful of countries where the majority of Jews is native-born. Stated another way, most Jews live in other than their native countries and may, as a result, have less verbal communication between first and third generations than is the case with any other peoples of the world. When grandparents and grandchildren do not fully master the same language, the role of the middle generation is more problematic.

8. While Jews remain primarily an urban people, there is growing evidence worldwide of a movement to smaller urban areas away from the larger cities. This creates a crisis in many Jewish community agencies and organizations which are not easily able to replicate and offer a comprehensive network of cultural, educational, and social services in these areas of new growth.

9. Other than in the United States and the British Isles, a high proportion of diaspora families of European descent has been scarred by the Holocaust. As a consequence, attitudes toward children, the forming of second families, memories of the martyred, guilt feelings of the survivors, and the remembrance of past horrors - all impinge upon family members in different ways with a volatility and impact which nonaffected families cannot truly comprehend.

10. The percentage of working women within the Jewish population seems to be increasing worldwide at a greater rate than

among non-Jewish women. This is a result of both economic necessity and growing opportunities for women with higher education to enter the work force at more advanced levels of complexity and professionalism.

The feminist movement is at its peak in many of the Western countries where Jews reside. As in the past, when radical attitudinal changes have taken place in a society, the middle class is often at the forefront in the expression of these changes. Such seems to be the case among a disproportionately high number of Jewish women. This trend is at the heart of the conflicting "role expectations" which modernity and Judaism place upon women and helps explain the changing nature of family formation, birthrates, and family structure.

11. Well over half the working Jews outside of Israel -- in some cases as many as 80 percent -- are managers, professionals, or business people, and thus tend to be linked to middle class aspirations and values, both in Western and Eastern European countries.

12. In almost all instances, Jews are at the upper socioeconomic level within their respective countries and as a result have a greater stake in the maintenance of the status quo. Countries with stable political regimes are thus seen by Jews as desirable places to live. Destabilization of the status quo rather than distaste for authoritarian regimes, per se, contributes to Jewish mobility to a greater degree than is often appreciated. Furthermore, there is a marked neutralization of perceived demographic differences between Jews and non-Jews when the differences are based upon socioeconomic variables; upper class Jews are demographically and economically more comparable to upper class non-Jews than to Jews in lower socioeconomic groups.

13. Most Jews throughout the world draw more frequently and extensively upon Western secular values to shape their lifestyles than upon Jewish values or sources. It appears that while most Jews and Jewish families spend the bulk of their free hours with other Jews, there is little to distinguish them as _Jewish_ families in their behavior vis-a-vis the general non-Jewish population in their respective countries of residence.

14. Much of the "new" phenomena identified among contemporary Jewish families is not as new as commonly believed. In spite of efforts to romanticize the Jewish family of old, there is a growing body of research suggesting that wife abuse, child abuse, and alcoholism are not only increasing today but were more prevalent in times past than has been acknowledged. The scope of these phenomena in contemporary Jewish families everywhere, including Israel, is far more extensive than generally recognized.

In summary, it is important not to overlook the following data when reviewing recent literature on the family in Western civilization: 1) Until the nineteenth century enlightenment, the Jewish family had a different primary purpose than the non-Jewish family; 2) The existence of the extended family was more often a projection of imagination than a reality; 3) The percentage of single-parent families a century ago was not markedly different than now, even though the causes are different today; 4) The downward shift in family size is not a new phenomenon in Western Europe; 5) The issue of values and their changing importance has produced a transnational, transethnic, and transreligious revolution for most inhabitants of the Western world.

BACKGROUND

The Jewish Family

In the pre-emancipation era, Jews were not treated as individuals but were dealt with as members of corporate entities. Historians (9) have noted the serendipitous result of this treatment: the outcome was the creation of a sophisticated and comprehensive network of social, welfare, educational, legal, and quasi-governmental services maintained by the Jewish community -- often semi-autonomous -- which nourished the family by actively affirming the traditional Jewish value system. The family and the community mutually reinforced common goals, values, and aspirations, resulting in an inextricable bonding of private behavior and expectations. Through teachings and actions both community and family prescribed and proscribed behaviors for all their members. Culturally accepted norms for child-rearing, parental and intergenerational roles, and language -- in short the very minutiae of every waking moment -- were part of an unbroken lifestyle which was sustained to and from the doorpost of the home to the doorstep of the synagogue.

It was ironic that these separate Jewish communal institutions and obligations, which provided structure for value transmission within the Jewish community, came into existence as a result of external definition and/or denigration (anti-Semitism) in the larger society. The phenomenon of Jewish segregation in pre-eighteenth-nineteenth century Europe forced the community to develop its own schools, courts, and social services. All was not rosy in shtetl, dorf, and ghetto, but Jews were involved in individual or familial lifestyles that differed in their constellation of expectations and roles from those of non-Jews.

Even as differences are noted, a caution must be exercised lest the over-romanticization of the past colors its reality. Gershon Cohen has stated, "The Jewish family never sustained the Jew....The family as a unit, in a strongly organized community, had very little to do except to generate, feed, and clothe kids. The community educated them...in the street, in the marketplace, in the synagogue, in the house of study, in the assembly hall." (10) Whether or not this is too simple an assessment, the irony was that the premodern Western non-Jewish family regarded itself, and was seen by society, much more as an economic unit than as one engaged in the transmission of values. Each family typically taught roles to its children, but the expectation for families to transmit moral values and ethical behavior was mostly a post-industrial phenomenon. Needless to say, the surrounding society always influenced Jewish expectations, values, and behavior.

The age-old struggle to survive as Jews was renewed when the coming of the emancipation to Europe in the late eighteenth century allowed the large majority of Jewish families to enter into Western society (Russia being the major exception prior to the Bolshevik Revolution). Jews sought to share in the Western world's growing emphasis on material acquisition resulting from the Industrial Revolution. The drive to attain the fruits of that revolution became for some a drive which overpowered the desire to remain Jews.

By the nineteenth century, the values and aspirations of Jews and non-Jews moved increasingly toward indistinguishable paths. The Jew (and in this instance the Jewish family) was often the prefigure and paradigm for what would come later in Western society. It is one thing to be the "drum major" for the Western world, but it is not possible to continue as such if the drumbeat is sounded as part of an orchestration of Western themes. The Jew's ability to survive results in large measure from an ability to accommodate to the tempo of a host society, while continuing to dance and march to the unique rhythm of Jewish time and Jewish cycles.

Many realities reflecting the changes in the West were most evident in America, for the new continent became the place of renewal for tens of millions from all corners of the earth. In America, the extended family was the "historical exception" and as Griswold points out, "rarely more than one-fifth of families (from the seventeenth century to the present) were extended in nature." (11) For the last 300 years, with rare exceptions, at least 40 percent of families in America have been nuclear; the Jewish family has been no exception.

Another phenomenon must be put into historical perspective: the rate of divorce has risen dramatically in the twentieth century. Yet in the United States the proportion of disrupted marriages was approximately the same in 1970 as in 1890; the increased number of divorces "almost exactly balanced out improvement in life expectancy." (12) Death of a spouse in 1890 -- the most important cause of single-parent families -- accounted for disrupted marriages to the same degree that divorce does today. As O'Neill has pointed out, "divorce (instead of death) is the safety valve which makes the modern family possible." (13) (Interestingly, the divorce rate in Palestine among Jews from 1935-1939 equalled the divorce rate among Americans in 1970 (Table I, below.)

Table I   Divorce Rate Per 1000

	United States 1970	Pales. 1935-3
Divorce Per 1,000 people	15	15.5

Source: America - Griswold
        Israel - R. Bachi

FUNCTIONS OF THE FAMILY

Most experts on the family today agree that during its life cycle the family must meet five developmental tasks. They are: 1) provision for security and physical survival; 2) provision for emotional and social functioning; 3) provision for sexual differentiation and training of children; 4) provision for support and growth of individual families; 5) provision for care of aging/dependent parents by children.(A) The fulfillment of these tasks represents not only the function of a fully healthy or "coping" family, but may be considered the minimal expectation of what a family should do. It is not by chance that no provision is made for value formation or transmission of religious beliefs as necessary family tasks. If anything, it indicates how minimalistic the expectations for family functions have become.

To confirm the changing nature of what was and is expected of family, one prominent psychotherapist analyzed the psychiatric literature of the 1960s and early 1970s to access the frequency with which various goals in family therapy were enunciated as important. He found that concern for the individual was widely expressed. While most people preferred "formal family life" to alternative lifestyles, most of these preferences were cast in the context of a nuclear family with little concern voiced for the extended family.(B) One likely consequence of this value framework is progressively less concern for the importance of traditional family tasks such as taking care of one's aging parents.

Lasch has suggested that following the political turmoil of the 1960s most Americans have become increasingly occupied with themselves. With no hope of bettering their lives in meaningful ways, he concludes, "people have convinced themselves that what matters is psychological self-improvement, getting in touch with their feelings, eating health food, taking lessons in ballet or belly dancing, immersing themselves in the wisdom of the East, learning how to 'relate,' overcoming the 'fear of pleasure.' (14)

Gerald B. Bubis

emphasis on self was encouraged by numerous psychologists, of whom now regret what they see as an overemphasis on the ual at the expense of the family. One outcome is the menon of young adults who are seen as not taking their own nting obligations seriously. "We psychologists have been re-nsible for this to a certain degree with our stress on self-tualization and realizing one's potential. This business of 'doing your wn thing' is...inimical to the notion of commitment to a child." (15)

On the other hand, there are those who would argue that the family cannot possibly accomplish what is expected of it as a unit. It is wrongly being called upon "to replace community, to provide leisure, love, respect, satisfaction, fulfillment...[which can only be done] as a community." (16)

This conflict between expectation and reality seems to have produced two prototypical families in America -- the "New Breed Parents" and the "Traditional Parents" -- who place differing emphases on the values held as important (Table II). "New Breed" parents tend to be the younger and better educated parents in America today. They tend toward a more permissive approach in child rearing than do the traditionalists, using less punishment and threats, being less concerned about children eating or going to bed at a set time, while being highly concerned about the health of the child from a psychic and physical point of view. There tends to be a greater degree of concern for children's autonomy, personal freedom, and freedom of choice than among "traditionalist" parents.

Numerically the "new breed" outweigh the "traditionalists" in the current parenting generation. As a result, the majority of this parenting generation de-emphasizes the values of money, work, family, religion, marriage, and service to others -- instead transmitting attitudes which clash with traditional middle class values historically associated with Western Jewish families. The number of "new breeds" increases as the level of education increases, so -- on the basis of Jewish commitment to educational activity -- it can be presumed that Jews are disproportionately represented in this group.

Hartman identifies four major threats to the family as: 1) technology; 2) revolutionary universalism; 3) despair; and 4) radical individualism, with the change from traditional values into emphasis on the self reflected in the last of the four. By technology, Hartman means the proclivity of Western society to value the new and discard the old -- resulting in a permanent state of dissatisfaction, and leading to loss of the family's function as the central institution. He feels that "parents are [only] significant when past is important." The result of "child-centeredness" is a future-oriented outlook, without

Table II   PERSONAL VALUES
              New Breed Versus Traditionalist Parents

Consider very important values:

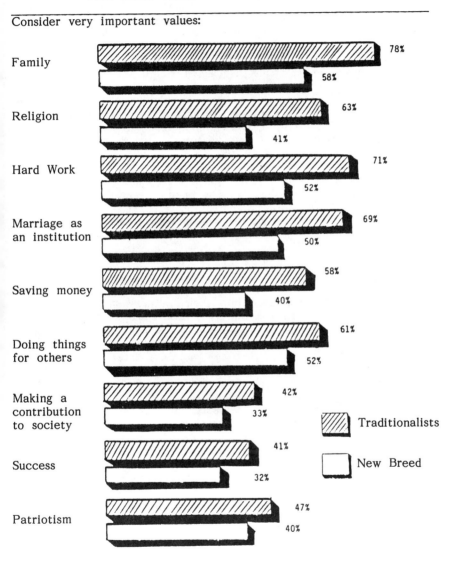

Family — 78% / 58%

Religion — 63% / 41%

Hard Work — 71% / 52%

Marriage as an institution — 69% / 50%

Saving money — 58% / 40%

Doing things for others — 61% / 52%

Making a contribution to society — 42% / 33%

Success — 41% / 32%

Patriotism — 47% / 40%

Traditionalists

New Breed

From Yankelovich -- General Mills Family Report, 1977.

the connection to past (tradition and history) that a "parent-centered" family offers. (17)   Hartman speaks of the transition of Jews from being a people with memories and customs to a people developing a more generalized approach to life in the present with little reference to time past. He calls this "revolutionary universalism," which he feels is accompanied by an all-pervasive despair. (18) (This is not borne out by the Yankelovitch study which found 88 percent of parents very or fairly optimistic about themselves and the future.) (19)

The most demonstrable change is the weakened sense of community. Even as one can conclude that a kind of tribal bonding is still, theoretically, the major "glue" for most people today; paradoxically, ethnicity and its chemistry are no longer as easily felt, transmitted, nor utilized as in the past. If, as Rosenberg suggests, "Judaism represents order, and Western culture represents feeling and emotion," (20) then the removal of order whose survival is only possible within the discipline of community creates more potential harm than communal workers appreciate. Elsewhere, I have argued that communal workers themselves are but reflections and products of the dominant non-Jewish society, and hold values formed by their respective dominant cultures - be they French, English, Canadian, American, Russian, Israeli, etc. (21)

Formerly, individuals did not generate cultural goals because those aspirations were infused into their cultures' institutions. Today we face an unusually radical and pervasive change which Maruyama calls a "metatransition." Because we are, worldwide, a temporarily goal-less society, we switch from traditional sources of goal orientation to other, more fleeting sources. Contemporary societies ultimately need to evolve healthy sub-units likened to the traditional gesellschaft. (22) Webster's abridged dictionary defines gesellschaft as an associative and rationally developed type of social relationship characterized by impersonally contracted associations between people, while the gemeinschaft is a spontaneously arising set of social relationships characterized by reciprocal bonds of sentiment and kinship with a common code of tradition.

The gesellschaft is an identifiable group which accommodates to individual variations while allowing dissatisfied members to leave and, by implication, others to enter.   The traditional Jewish community was and is structured along the lines of a gemeinschaft, where those who are "in" tend to be self-enveloped and self-enveloping.   Consequently it is difficult to escape and even harder to enter. (23)

Most Jews have broken from the gemeinschaft. They are now adrift. While some do return to the certitude provided by the traditional Jewish community (the ba'alei t'shuva are one example), the majority seem to draw at least some tentative satisfaction, and greater comfort at best, in just identifying themselves as Jews without the need to do anything other than "feel Jewish." Some wish to recreate the gesellschaft as they seek old-new ways to link themselves to a community which they can enter and leave as it suits them. Loosely structured and impersonal organizations geared to social action and focused on Jewish concerns would appeal to this group.

Jung was reputed to have said, "Those who 'belonged' didn't have to see me for therapy, and I was never able to cure those who never felt they belonged." Most modern Jews, along with their non-Jewish contemporaries, seem to have long ceased to fathom or value the wisdom of Jung's insight. The clash between Judaism and modern Western values is the context within which today's Jews find themselves. Their tension arises from trying either to choose between or to combine the two. The whirlpool of values and options available to the modern Jew push and pull. They are themselves contradictory and produce contradictory actions and reactions. We are better able to confront this problem by perceiving and examining the behaviors of Jews as they manifest their Westernized values. As professionals, we must not only understand the trends but, more importantly, evolve workable strategies in responding to them.

III

DEMOGRAPHIC DATA

This section presents available demographic data on Jews throughout the world, detailing the thumbnail sketch in section I of this monograph. Israel will be dealt with separately because it is, of course, the only place in the world where the social policies of the Jewish community evolve from and are defined by a government rather than by voluntary consent of a sector of the society.

Classically, a number of demographic categories have been utilized as the context for understanding the founding and continuity of the Jewish family. Such data, from which conclusions can be drawn and projections made, include rates of marriage, fertility, death, intermarriage, along with socioeconomic and educational levels.

Before the nineteenth century the majority of Jews lived in Eastern Europe. Given the inaccessibility of data, as well as the inconsistency of the studies which are available, Bachi's sources (24) seem to be the most comprehensive and reliable for that period.

At the beginning of the nineteenth century, there were approximately 2.5 million Jews in the world out of a total population of approximately one billion. (25) During the nineteenth and early twentieth centuries, Jews had a higher birthrate than the balance of the world's population including the then developed countries. (26) As a result, by the start of the twentieth century, there were 10.7 million Jews in the world. While the peak number of 16.3 million was reached in 1939, before the Holocaust, the rate of growth had already decelerated. (27) Subsequent to the Holocaust, the Jewish population continued to decrease, so that, today, best estimates indicate that there are 13 million Jews in the world, (28) of whom approximately 3.4 million reside in Israel. (29) (Table III)

The demographic profile of Eastern European Jewry in the early nineteenth century was of a bonded community with high marriage rates; low mixed marriage rates; few spinsters; early marriages the norm; high remarriage rates among the widowed and divorced (more common than often realized); large families; relatively few out-of-wedlock births; and pregnancy often the norm until menopause. The average size family probably had seven children. (30) The same patterns seem to have been evident among Jews in Near Eastern and North African countries in the nineteenth century as well. (31)

Wrigley has shown that as long ago as the late fourteenth century in England, small families resulting from late marriages

14   Gerald B. Bubis

Table III   WORLD JEWISH POPULATION ESTIMATES   (1975)
In Thousands

Region Country	Estimates by Schmelz	Estimates by the American Jewish Year Book (rounded)	Difference (2) - (3)
(1)	(2)	(3)	(4)
DIASPORA			
America, total [a]	6,417	6,772	-355
U.S.A.	5,600	5,840 (1972: 6,115)[e]	-240(-515)[e]
Canada	295	305	-10
Argentina	265	300 (1972: 500)[e]	-35(-235)[e]
Brazil	110	165	-55
Other countries	147	162	-15
Europe, [b] total	1,316	1,374	-58
France	535	550 (1976: 650)[e]	-15(-115)[e]
United Kingdom	400	410	-10
Other countries	381	414	-33
U.S.S.R. [c]	1,950	2,680	-720
Asia [d]	88	105	-17
Africa, total	177	184	-7
South Africa, Rhodesia	120	123	-3
Other countries	57	61	-4
Oceania	72	77	-5
DIASPORA, TOTAL	10,020	11,192	-1,172 (1,747)
ISRAEL	2,959	2,953	+6
WORLD	12,979	14,145	-1,166 (1,741)

a) The AJYB estimate for 1975 includes non-Jewish household
   members of Jews: Schmelz's estimate excludes them.
b) Excluding U.S.S.R., including European territories of Turkey.
c) Based on census results which may underrepresent the Jewish
   population of USSR (the AJYB estimate is based on the 1959
   censuses).
d) Excluding U.S.S.R., including Asian territories of Turkey.
e) Estimates given in volumes of the American Jewish Year Book,
   prior to 1975.
Source: The Demographic Crisis of Diaspora Jewry, Roberto Bachi

constituted a pattern among a significant minority of the population. Nuclear families were predominant as early as the seventeenth century, with a marked drop noted in the birthrate. He traces patterns of difference between Western and Eastern Europe, demonstrating that the American patterns referred to earlier (of small size nuclear families) were prefigured in Western Europe. This now provides the general societal framework for most Jews today. (32)

By the early twentieth century these marked Western trends also existed among Jews. Not the least of these trends were: 1) later marriage among Jews than the general population; 2) a substantial number of Jewish women, especially in Central Europe, never marrying; 3) a significant number of "out-marriages" and/or conversions of convenience to Christianity for economic or societal reasons. (33)

The worldwide contemporary demographic trends have been ably analyzed by Schmelz. He points out that eighty percent of today's Jews live in lands which housed only three percent of world Jewry 100 years ago - namely Israel, the Americas, South Africa, and Australia. (34) From Schmelz's data and studies by others, the following profile of diaspora Jewry may be drawn: 1) very high urbanization; 2) high and increasing level of formal education; 3) high percentage of individuals in white collar positions, including a high percentage in professional and managerial positions; 4) long life expectancy; 5) decreasing fertility rate; 6) increasing proportion of nonmarrieds; 7) increasing proportion of late-marrieds; 8) rising percentage of divorce. (35)

An analysis of the demographers' research reveals patterns found throughout the diaspora. In South Africa, the pattern of Jewish intermarriage rates is comparable to that of the United States even though rabbis in South Africa do not perform mixed marriages. (36) Though the percentage rate is slightly lower, the pattern is in keeping with findings in the United States. (37) Dubb feels, as do many in the United States, that some Jews with spouses who are not converted will bring up their children as Jews and that Jewish/ non-Jewish intermarriage does not lead inevitably to loss of the Jewish partner and his or her children from the Jewish community. (38)

In his studies of American Jewish fertility patterns, Della Pergola concludes:

1) The fertility of American Jews has been consistently lower than that of other Caucasians since the beginning of this century.

Gerald B. Bubis

TABLE IV RATES OF NATURAL MOVEMENT AMONG JEWS AND GENERAL POPULATION, BY COUNTRY AND PERIOD
(Per 1,000 of Population)

Country	Period	Birth Rate		Death Rate		Rate of Natural Increase/Decrease	
		Jews[a]	Gen. Pop.	Jews	Gen. Pop.	Jews[a]	Gen. Pop.
U.S.A.	1967–71	10	17[b]	10	9.5[b]	0	7.5[b]
Canada	1957–61	17	27	7	8	10	19
	1967–71	12	17	10	7	2	10
Sao Paulo (Brazil)	1965–69	10		7		3	
Argentina	1956–60	11	24	10	9	1	15
South Africa	1966–70	16	23[b]	9	9[b]	7	14[b]
Australia	1957–61	14	23	9	9	5	14
	1967–71	11	20	11	9	0	11
Greater Paris	1972–76[c]	9	15	9	9	0	6
Origin of Jews:							
Europe		9		12		–3	
Africa-Asia		9		7		2	

Brussels (Belgium)	1957–61	8	13	10	13	−2	0
Netherlands	1962–66	11	19	13	8	−2	11
Germany (Fed. Rep.)	1961–65	3	18	21	11	−18	7
	1971–75	3	11	19	12	−16	−1
Switzerland	1959–62	11	18	16	10	−5	8
	1969–72	12	15	16	9	−4	6
Italy	1961–65	11	19	16	10	−5	9
	1966–70	11	17	15	10	−4	7
Russian Republic (in Soviet Union)	1959–70	6	18	15	8	−9	10
Israel (Jews)	1971–75	24		7		17	
Origin of Jews: Europe	1975	21		10		11	
Africa-Asia	1975	29		5		24	

a "Effectively Jewish" rates; see text.
b Whites.
c Averages for the 5-year interval preceding the years indicated.
Sources and methods: see Appendix.

Gerald B. Bubis

Table V

Jewish Marriage Rates and Current Frequencies of Mixed Marriages among Selected Jewish Populations in Europe, 1958–1977.

Place	Years	Marriage rates		% mixed marriages[d]		
		Jewish population	General population	Out of all couples involving at least one Jewish spouse	Out of couples with Jewish grooms	Out of couples with Jewish brides
(1)	(2)	(3)	(4)	(5)	(6)	(7)
AUSTRIA						
Vienna	1961–65	3[a]	9	72	67	34
	1966–70	3[a]	9	63	54	34
	1971–75	3[a]	7	55	42	34
DENMARK	1968			75		
Copenhagen	1960–64	5[a]	8[e]			
	1965–69	6[a]	8[e]			
FRANCE						
Strasbourg	1960–66			29		
Paris	1965–74			42	31	33
GERMANY, F.R.	1961–65	3[b]	8	81	78	43
	1966–70	2[b]	7	74	67	45
	1971–75	2[b]	6	78	69	57
GREAT BRIT I	1961–65	4[a]	8		–	
	1966–70	4[a]	8			–
	1971–75	4[a]	8			
	1976	3[a]				
ITALY	1961–65	5[a]	8			
	1966–70	4[a]	7			
	1971–75	4[a]	8			
Rome	1961–65	7[a]	8	21[i]	13[i]	10[i]
	1966–70	6[a]	7	20[i]	15[i]	8[i]
	1971–75	6[a]	7	43[j]		
Milan	1961–65	4[a]	7	50	45	28
	1966–70	3[a]	7	60	53	28
	1971–75	3[a]	6	70	57	50
	1976			57	45	33
6 Medium commun.	1961–65	3[a]	8[f]			
	1966–70	2[a]	7[f]			
	1971–75	2[a]	8[f]			

Place (1)	Years (2)	Marriages rates		% mixed marriages[d]		
		(3)	(4)	(5)	(6)	(7)
15 Small commun.	1961–65	2[a]	8[f]			
	1966–70	3[a]	7[f]			
	1971–75	2[a]	8[f]			
LUXEMBOURG	1959–70	4[a]	6	34		
	1971–76	3	6			
NETHERLANDS	1958–67			61	48	39
Amsterdam	1960–64			56	43	35
SWEDEN						
Stockholm	1972–75	4[a]	5[g]			
	1976–77	3[a]	..			
Malmoe	1966–68	2[a]	7[g]			
	1972–76	4[a]	5			
Goeteborg	1966–68	3[a]	7[g]			
SWITZERLAND	1961–65	3[b]	7	58	49	31
	1966–70	4[b]	7	56	44	26
	1971–75	3[b]	6	61	45	42
	1976	3[b]	6	61	45	42
Zurich	1961–65	5[b]	11	43	37	14
	1966–70	5[b]	10	36	26	17
	1971–75	4[b]	9	44	28	27
TURKEY	1968–70	7[c]				
	1972–75	5[c]				
Izmir	1961–65	6[a]	8[h]			
	1966–70	8[a]				
	1971–75	8[a]				

(a) Jewish community records: marriages performed with a Jewish ceremony.

(b) Official statistics: marriages between Jews regardless of type of ceremony.

(c) Official statistics: marriages of Jews regardless of religion of partner.

(d) Official statistics: unadjusted for marriage celebrated only with Jewish religious ceremony and lacking civil validigy.

(e) Denmark.

(f) Italy.

(g) Sweden.

(h) Turkey.

(i) Provisional estimates: records linkage of Jewish community and general civil status registers. Further cases of mixed marriages performed in past years may still be found.

(j) Indirect estimate, based on the number of Jewish births to non-Jewish mothers.

Gerald B. Bubis

2) Basically, Jewish fertility levels follow general fluctuations, but patterns of response to periodic societal changes were perceived earlier - thus foreshadowing and moving sooner in the direction of increasingly lower fertility.

3) Marriages have tended to occur later in life and resulting fertility patterns have been consistent - that is, there has been a lower birthrate than in the general population.

4) There seems to be a minimum level of reproduction below which Jewish families seem unwilling to fall, providing "societal circumstances are not too exacting" - for example, economic distress and war.

5) The age at marriage does not have any marked effect on family size in the sense that late marrieds tend to have the same number of children as those who married young. (39)

In discussing the current population of Western Europe, it is to be noted that the total European Jewish population is about 3.2 million -- of which one-third is in Western Europe and two-thirds in Eastern Europe. (40) In Western Europe the two great Jewish population clusters are to be found in and around Paris and London. Different factors influence mobility of Jews in Europe as compared to the mobility of American Jews. In Europe it has been demonstrated that: "Towns with a wide range of commercial, financial, administrative, and cultural activities may be more attractive for Jews than larger industrial towns whose economic setting is less differentiated [...because of] the peculiar structure of the Jewish labor force and also of a strong Jewish need for higher learning and sophisticated cultural opportunities. Public admin- istration centers as such lack a great potential for attracting Jews since the latter's numbers as public servants are usually relatively small." (41) Fewer Jews are involved in the civil service infrastructure of European countries than in the United States and South Africa. (42) Thus, in Europe, the linkage to long-time urban Jewish quarters is still a factor, though a diminishing one, in attracting Jewish settlement.

In all of Western Europe there are only 28 metropolitan areas with at least 5,000 Jews. Eight are in England and eight in France; two each in Belgium, Italy, and West Germany; one each in Turkey, the Netherlands, Sweden, Austria, Switzerland, and Denmark. These include 80 percent of all the Jews in Western Europe. (43) Additional factors affecting population patterns include the general socio- economic characteristics of the area, the availability of housing, especially at times of high Jewish immigration, and the availability of Jewish schools, synagogues, and the like. (44)

Community is weakening among the young as they become more and more physically dispersed. As a result, there is a lower rate of communal affiliation, with fewer considering themselves as part of Jewish life in any organized way. These trends are highly parallel to those in the United States, with some minor variations which can be found in a country by country comparison. The tables which accompany this analysis disclose these parallel developments and are almost interchangeable throughout the diaspora. A number of these descriptions fit the majority of Jews in Israel. However, developments unique to Israel and the United States can be delineated as well.

IV

THE UNITED STATES AND ISRAEL

In the United States, all of the trends identified in the last section as present in diaspora communities exist (with the exceptions previously noted) especially with reference to the impact and import of the Holocaust.

The remarkable consistency of the various family patterns in question has been noted. Nuclear families -- small in number, well educated, upwardly mobile, on the move physically, Jewishly illiterate, long lived with substantial rates of mixed marriage -- are shared phenomena in nearly all diaspora communities. Some of these trends are now to be seen in Israel as well.

Two additional phenomena seem to be unique in the degree to which they are evident in the United States. The first is the extent of homosexuality among Jews. It is now quite clear that a substantial minority of Jewish men and women in the United States are avowed homophiles. There is a growing possibility that more males than females are homosexual, which means that fewer Jewish males are available for heterosexual marriage. At the same time, preliminary research suggests that a growing minority of Jewish homophiles desires to establish some kind of Jewish family lifestyle and in some instances this includes the desire to be parents. (45)

The second attribute particular to the U.S. seems to be the extent of the existence of four generation families. This temporary reality has importance for the present and implications for the near future, because one generation is often called upon to give major or supplemental economic support to the other three generations. This seems to result in a shift in priorities for the involved families which has been particularly exacerbated by the inflationary pressures of the American economy.

Discretionary income which once may have been earmarked for Jewish and general contributions will probably be used for serving the needs of the four generations to an increasing degree in the next decade. One might conclude that the increased costs attendant upon caring for all four generations might account for a substantial percentage of the shrinking numbers affiliated with and/or supporting Jewish institutions and causes in America.

While many of the phenomena identified in the diaspora are also found in Israel, there exist unique differences. A "thumbnail" profile of Israel's Jewish families reveals the following:

23

1. Extended families are to be found more frequently in Israel than in the diaspora. Further, the size of the country results in more frequent occasions for family members to come together, to be affected by, and to affect, each other. Intergenerational values, while changing, are not as radically different as they are in the diaspora.

2. While Jews in Israel represent approximately twenty to twenty-five percent of the world Jewish population, approximately forty percent of all Jewish babies born annually are born in Israel. Even so, the birthrate in Israel is on a downward trend and as early as the 1920s and 1930s, Jewish demographers identified this as a, or possibly, the major concern for all Jews and a concern of highest priority for the Jewish state whenever it would come into existence. (46).

3. Marriage in Israel, while still at an earlier age than elsewhere, is moving in the direction of diaspora Jewish marriages, with a pattern of later marriages being more discernible than in the past.

4. While the Jewish community in Israel has a younger median age than any other Jewish community in the world, the aging population in Israel is causing major dislocations. Israel was built by the young for the young and will be faced with the impact of aging upon family and physical structures in the next decade and a half. The kibbutzim and moshavim are being forced to adapt to a generation of elders whose presence was largely unanticipated by the founders. (In urban environments, there will probably be problems for older family members living in the upper floors of apartment buildings where there are no elevators.)

5. When compared to Jews elsewhere, the Jews of Israel present an anomaly vis-a-vis their socioeconomic status. As previously mentioned, the educational level of Jews in the diaspora has placed them primarily in an upper socioeconomic status with a dispro- portionately high percentage being in the managerial, professional, or business classes. Projections suggest that this percentage will increase slightly or at least be maintained everywhere except in Israel. (47)

In Israel, internal economic and sociological realities will result in a reversal of this trend. Currently, 80 percent of Israeli Jews hold managerial, professional, or business positions. However, a sig- nificantly smaller percentage of Israeli Jews attend universities compared with Jews elsewhere. Of those attending, the greater percentage by far ·are of Ashkenazi origin -- now the numerical minority in Israel -- while the large majority entering the labor force early are edot hamizrah (Jews of Oriental origin). Because they enter as workers in skilled and unskilled positions, and continue to gain in numerical superiority, they tilt downward the total percentages working in the so-called middle and upper class positions. It is projected that by 1990 only 60 percent of employed Israeli Jews will be engaged in managerial, professional, or business occupations as compared to 80 percent at present. The economic position of those in "blue collar" positions will probably exceed the "white collar" groups, but problems of status and social power will remain. (48) This will have a great effect upon the nature of the Jewish family in Israel and may also be a source of increased polarization between Israel and diaspora Jewry. Religious, cultural, and socioeconomic differences will continue to include linguistic differences as well; thus the sense of interdependence and shared commonality of outlook and concern between Israelis and diaspora Jews may be further minimized.

6. Jews in Israel are increasingly urbanized but the trends seen elsewhere toward suburban and smaller urban centers are also in evidence. One result of this may be that the efforts of Project Renewal to reverse the effects of urban blight will become increasingly important. Thus, the current five year limit on implementation of Project Renewal projects may severely limit the much needed benefits resulting from successful Project Renewal programs.

7. The rate of divorce in Israel is on the rise. This is another index of a parallel trend linking Jews in the developed countries with those elsewhere. (While the divorce rate is lower within the Orthodox community, there is preliminary evidence in America indicating a marked increase in divorce rates among observant Jews. This could lead one to speculate that the differences in divorce rates among various Jewish groups may well narrow in the future.)

8. As would be expected, of all Jewish communities in the world, the mixed marriage rate is lowest in Israel. There is, however, a small but discernible upward trend in mixed marriages between Arabs and Jews which historically is not a new phenomenon. While outside of Israel the majority of mixed marriages involve Jewish men, the tendency is the opposite in Israel. As long as the environmental opportunities for cultural and social contacts are minimal, as seems to be the case in Israel, the mixed marriage rate should remain remarkably low. Outside of Israel, however, the Jew who marries a non-Jew is not inevitably "lost" to the Jewish community and, as noted previously, in some countries a large minority of children of mixed marriages is raised as Jews. In Israel, this is seldom the case, because the non-Jew rarely converts to Judaism. Thus, the rate of loss to the Jewish community is higher.

9. In Israel, the ramifications of mobility are of a different nature than is the case in the diaspora. The bulk of olim (immigrants to Israel) in the last thirty years came as family units. Few people in the past thirty years moved to Israel for the ideological reasons which often split families asunder in earlier days. The mass evacuation of Jews from the Arab countries in the 1950s accounts for Israel's present Sephardi majority. This movement created, almost overnight, a society of extended families in a country of singles and nuclear families, for the prestate halutzim (pioneers) came to Palestine with few three-generational families among them.

The recent phenomenon of yerida (emigration) has brought to the fore the realities of mobility and its impact upon the Israeli family. It has been estimated that most Israelis living abroad visit Israel at least once every three years. The national policy requiring army service of those who move abroad will undoubtedly cause more and more difficulties for those families who cannot visit outside of Israel because of economic reasons. One can but conjecture what the long term psychological and emotional consequences may be as the intense family ties so frequently associated with Israel are attenuated as a result of government policy and continuing emigration. If Israelis in Israel cannot afford to travel and Israelis outside are not clear of their status when visiting Israel, a new split may result.

10. As in most countries of the world, a large percentage of Israeli women is in the work force. As is also the case in most socialist countries, the government has provided many benefits which encourage women to have children while remaining in the work force. At the same time, attitudes toward women in Israel are much more traditional than in most Western countries and this ambivalence becomes apparent when one analyzes the percentage of women in various fields of endeavor. In Israel, still a developing country, economic realities, combined with attitudinal realities, account for much more "traditional" expectations of what is "proper" woman's work. Further compounding the inconsistencies is the high illiteracy rate among Jewish women from Arab countries. This helps account for the greater proportion of Israeli women in unskilled jobs.

11. Little comprehensive research has yet appeared on rates of child abuse, wife abuse, and alcoholism in Israel. Discussions with, and estimates by, counsellors, social workers, and other officials suggest that the rates may be as high as in the diaspora.

12. Finally, Israel has not been immune to the trend toward secularization and, as elsewhere, outside of strongly observant enclaves, the family has often absorbed the best and the worst of Western secular values in commerce, culture, and family life styles.

In sum, Israel is the only place in the world except South Africa (49) where Jews are still experiencing a substantial rate of growth; the <u>overall</u> rate is decreasing so that the population in Israel is also aging. While the rates of change in Israel are much slower than in diaspora Jewry, there is a trend toward fewer marriages, a rise in the age of those marrying, an increasing number of unmarried couple households, an increase in the proportion of births out of wedlock, and an increase in divorce rates. (50)

Table VI   NUMBER OF DIVORCES IN ISRAEL

	MALES		FEMALES	
	1965-9	1970-74	1965-4	1970-4
Among marrying persons	7.2	6.1	6.4	4.6
Among divorcing persons	15.7	14.1	15.2	13.2

According to marital status prior to marriage being dissolved by divorce.

Table VII   MORTALITY

Life expectancy at birth in Israel for Jews

	MALE	FEMALE
1926-27	54.1	54.7
1973-75	70.7	73.6

Table VIII   LITERACY AND EDUCATION LEVELS IN ISRAEL

Years	Male	Female	Total
Percentage of Illiterates			
1931	5.7	22.5	14.1
1948	3.2	9.6	6.3
1956	8.2	21.7	15.0
1961	7.2	17.1	12.1
1972	5.9	12.9	9.2

Gerald B. Bubis

Table IX   DIVORCE

Yearly number of divorces among Jews per 1000 of each
sex aged 15 and over in Palestine and Israel

	Period	Male	Female
Palestine	1935-39	15.7	15.4
	1940-44	8.5	8.6
Israel	1948-49	4.5	4.2
	1950-54	5.1	4.9
	1955-59	4.4	3.6
	1960-64	3.1	3.1
	1965-69	2.7	2.7
	1970-72	2.6	2.6
	1973-75	2.7	2.6

Table X   AVERAGE ANNUAL NUMBER OF DIVORCES

Per 1000 households with each number of children (aged 0-1)

No. of Children	0	1	2	3	4	5	6 and over	TOTAL
1960-62	6.0	4.8	2.5	---------	1.1	--------------		4.1
1971-73	3.8	5.0	3.2	1.7	11.2	.10	0.5	3.4

This is but slight increase from 40.9% in 1955 to 47.6% in 1974 of the proportion of divorced couples with children.

Gerald B. Bubis

Table XI   PERCENTAGE OF RESPECTIVE POPULATION
                IN ISRAEL OVER 55 YEARS OF AGE

Period	Jews	Non-Jews
1960	12.9	8.9
1970	16.7	7.5
1978	17.5	6.3

Source: Jerusalem Post, January 26, 1981 quoting from
         publication, Society in Israel, 1980, Central
         Bureau of Statistics, Israel.

Table XII   FERTILITY RATES IN ISRAEL

Period	Jews	Non-Jews
1960	3.5	8.0
1978	2.8	6.2

Source: Ibid.

Table XIII PARTICIPATION RATE IN CIVILIAN LABOR FORCE OF JEWISH WOMEN, BY MARITAL STATUS

Number and Age of Children

A - In labor force per 100 of each age and marital status 1972-5

Marital Status	14-17	18-24	25-34	35-54	55-64	65+	All over 14
Unmarried	16.1	52.4	81.9	60.5	26.2	5.4	34.9
Married	20.0	39.3	38.1	37.5	23.5	6.7	33.6

B - In labor force per 100 non-single women of each age and with each number of children 1971-5

Age of Woman	No. of Children				Age of Youngest				All Non-single
	0	1	2	3+	0-1	2-4	5-9	10-13	
14-34	63.2	39.5	28.3	17.1	24.1	31.9	41.9	40.1	35.7
35-44	46.9	41.3	40.1	23.4	21.0	29.2	37.4	42.9	37.5
45 & over	21.2	31.7	23.0	17.0	x	x	25.7	19.6	22.7
All	27.9	37.9	24.3	20.6	25.1	32.0	37.1	37.2	29.7

x Too small a sample to calculate reliably.
Source: Bachi, p. 312.

Gerald B. Bubis

Table XIV   YEARS OF SCHOOLING

Percentage by number of years at school of persons
attending or who have attended school in Israel.

Year		Male	Female	Total
1961	1-4	8.0	9.2	8.6
	5-8	39.3	41.7	40.5
	9-12	39.8	39.6	39.6
	13+	12.9	9.5	11.3
1962	1-4	4.1	4.8	4.0
	5-8	31.9	33.1	32.5
	9-12	47.5	46.6	47.0
	13+	16.5	15.6	16.1

Median	Male	Female	Total
1961	8.9	7.9	8.4
1972	10.0	9.5	9.8

Table XV   LAST SCHOOL ATTENDED

Percentage by type of last school of person attending
or who have attended schools - 1972

	Male	Female	Total
Elementary	34.3	35.9	35.1
Intermediate	7.4	3.8	5.7
Vocational or Agricultural	21.5	14.1	17.9
Secondary	19.5	27.0	22.9
Post Secondary	2.1	8.0	5.0
University	11.0	7.5	9.3
Other	4.7	3.5	4.1

V

TRENDS

An Analysis

IMPACT ON THE FUTURE

Let us now return to a discussion of some of the trends which will engage those working with Jews in the decades ahead. The rates of mixed marriages throughout the world show a remarkable series of converging trends (51) (Table IV) and are related to both the physical mobility and the psychic identity of the Western Jew. All available data demonstrate an increased rate of mixed marriages. However, there are a number of demographers and sociologists who caution against arriving at extreme pessimistic conclusions from these data. (52) Goldscheider has responded specifically to some of the concerns raised by Bachi by citing the need for caution in that "intermarriage cannot always be viewed as a demographic loss to the Jewish community...[with] negative implications;" stating that his "analysis in the United States suggests the quantitative impact of intermarriage is much less significant in the United States than what has often been portrayed in both popular and 'scientific' publications." (53)

Nevertheless, the facts of intermarriage inevitably have consequences for the family as a unit. Elsewhere I have discussed the emotional and psychological ramifications of dealing with cultural conflicts and claims on ethnic loyalty growing out of the desire of nuclear mixed marrieds and intermarried families to emulate the lifestyle of their grandparents. (54) Christian grandparents will vie with Jewish grandparents in providing grandchildren with opportunities to celebrate Hanukkah and Christmas, Passover and Easter, and the like. Resulting psychological pressures emanating from both intermarried families and blended families formed by second marriages have also been discussed. The extent of the pressures upon and consequent ability of children to deal with two or more sets of parents and siblings is just beginning to be studied in a comprehensive way. A substantial minority of Jewish children outside of Israel now have both Christian and Jewish relatives, including siblings and parents, and are being raised and/or are living in conflicting religious environments, while all the family members are desirous of close and enduring familial contacts. Grandparents and parents may be at odds as to how children should be raised and the degree to which, if at all, Jewish identity and practice should be encouraged. This issue will be of increasing concern in the years to come.

Feminist attitudes, coinciding with the entry of women into the workplace, sharply affect many nontraditional Western Jews. These attitudes and expectations must be added to the list of demographic and psychological realities. This phenomenon in part explains the changing fertility rates, rates of marriage, and/or postponed marriages. Generally, participation in the workforce is a function of socioeconomic class (55) and in the United States, over 50 percent of women are now estimated to be working, with the proportion among Jews thought to be higher.

In Israel, the number and percentage of working women has soared; 27.9 percent of Jewish women in Israel were working in 1955, a figure which rose to 37.9 percent in 1978 while the percentage of Arab women working in Israel in the same period remained a constant 11.5 percent. (56)

The impact of Western values and behaviors continues to permeate the lifestyle of the Jewish family. Orthodox Jews, approximately one-fifth of Israel's Jewish population, are a much smaller proportion in the diaspora. While many of the trends discussed herein are less evident among traditional Jews than nontraditional Jews, there are data suggesting that traditional Jewish families are also being affected. For example, wife abuse is on the rise among Jews, and in Israel this is particularly the case among those identifying themselves as traditional Jews. Rasnik estimates that there are between 40,000-50,000 abused women in Israel and claims a disproportionately high percentage are from traditional families. (57) Much of this seems to be related to class and cultural background, being particularly high among the edot hamizrah (Jews of Oriental origin who emigrated from Arab lands) but others have also identified this trend among middle class Jews in America. (58)

Recent findings of Geller and Goldsmith that child abuse is much more prevalent among Jews than previously believed, is another symptom contradicting the often idealized model of the Jewish family. (59) Spiegel has confirmed the reality of alcoholism among a growing minority of Jews and demonstrates that this phenomenon was to be found in Europe in centuries past to a degree much greater than appreciated. (60)

In the attempt to delineate signs of trouble within Jewish families, radical demographic changes conspire to skew the percentages involved with identifying "normal families." Census data from North America make it quite clear that only a minority of people live in households where two parents and at least one child reside. (61) Yet of all the developments affecting the Jewish family throughout the world, none seems so widespread as the diminished size of families caused by the decreasing fertility rate among Jews.

From the mid-1960s to the mid-1970s, the absolute numbers of live births among Jews in most European countries were reduced 20 to 50 percent. (62) In the past, <u>drastic</u> rate drops have been associated with extraordinary events such as famine or depressions but in this instance, as in North America, the change stemmed from the independent decisions of young Jews. The rate is further affected by the decreasing numbers of those of child-bearing age. In Europe, for example, there are comparatively few people in the fertile age range which thus compounds the problem (Table XVII). European birthrates have been intrinsically low for a relatively long period as "the first typical Jewish demographic trait [in Europe] to disappear was the tendency to marry young." (63) Bachi reviews data showing that while 60 percent of Jewish brides in Russia between 1867 and 1872 married by age 20, by 1901 to 1906 only 24 percent were married by age 20; while in Poland, by the mid-1930s, only 3 to 4 percent of the Jewish women were married by age 20. Even more importantly, he shows an increasing trend by the mid-1930s of women in Eastern Europe, and especially in Central Europe, who did not marry at all. (64) Presently, in every country in Europe (Table XVIII) there is an average of less than two children in every Jewish family. This trend toward markedly fewer children has even been adopted in France by the younger North African immigrants. (65)

In America and Israel the single most common mark of differentiation between traditional and nontraditional Jewish communities remains that of self-identified traditional Jewish women having somewhat larger families than nontraditional Jews, even though Jews as a whole have fewer children than non-Jews as a whole. (66) The American pattern has been most comprehensively analyzed by Goldstein. (67) While the data are incomplete and some questions have been raised, the experts' consensus is that Jews are not reproducing themselves. The American Jewish fertility rates have consistently paralleled the general changes in America's fertility rates for the last century but always at a lower rate than for non-Jews. (68) The same pattern is demonstrable in Argentina, (69) Canada, (70) South Africa, (71) England, (72) and, as previously cited, throughout the rest of Europe, including Russia. (73)

A cautionary voice found in the literature is that of Calvin Goldscheider who argues that marital fertility rates and total fertility rates must be separated to understand what is really happening. He argues that Jewish families have tended to have two children since the 1920s and continue to do so. The seemingly lower rates in America, he argues, are due primarily to "changes in marriage patterns and the tempo of family formation rather than the ultimate family size of married Jewish couples." (74) However, the end result is the same and statistics appear virtually unanimous in showing that

Gerald B. Bubis

Table XVI

FERTILITY MEASURES[a] OF JEWS AND GENERAL POPULATION, BY COUNTRY AND PERIOD

Country	Period	Fertility Ratio			Total Fertility Rate		% Change[b]	
		Jews	Gen. Pop.	% Difference	Jews	Gen. Pop.	Jewish Births	Jewish Fertility Ratio
U.S.A.	1967–71	228	392c	−32	1.4	2.4c	−30	−41
Canada	1957–61	421	606	−30	2.6	3.7	−14	4
	1967–71	292	390	−25	1.8	2.3	−14	−30
Sao Paulo (Brazil)	1965–69	220			1.3		−38	−42
Argentina	1956–60	247	471	−48	1.5	2.8	−24	−22
South Africa	1966–70	387	476c	−19	2.4	3.1c,d	−1	−14
Australia	1957–61	353	528	−33	2.2	3.4	−16	8
	1967–71	296	460	−36	1.8	2.9	1	−20
Greater Paris	1972–76e	221	344	−36	1.4	2.0	−38	−44
Origin of Jews:								
Europe		257			1.6		−44	−44
Africa-Asia		199			1.2		−31	−43

Brussels (Belgium)	1957–61	238	322	−26	1.4	2.0	−31	−27
Netherlands	1962–66	302	406f	−26	1.8	3.0	8	4
Switzerland	1956–60	315	383	−18	1.9	2.3	−10	−3
	1966–70	305	364	−16	1.8	2.3	−5	−16
Italy	1961–65	303	398	−24	1.8	2.4	3	20
	1966–70	249	396	−37	1.5	2.4	−24	−37
Israel (Jews)	1971–75	529			3.2		18	−4
Origin of Jews:								
Europe	1975	492			2.8		30	8
Africa-Asia	1975	560			3.6		10	−12

aFor explanation of technical terms, see text. The measures for Jews relate to "effectively Jewish" fertility and births.
bPer cent change in interval between the two latest 5-year periods.
cWhites.
d1970 only.
eAverage for the 5-year interval(s) preceding the years indicated.
f1963–1967.

Table XVII

AVERAGE NUMBER OF CHILDREN BORN PER JEWISH WOMAN, BY AGE OF WOMEN, COUNTRY AND YEAR

Jewish Women, by Age at Enumeration

Age:	U.S.A. 1971	Canada 1961	Canada 1971	Argentina 1960	Australia 1966	Greater Paris 1972-76 Origin of Jews: Total	Europe	Africa-Asia	Netherlands 1966	Italy 1965	European Immigrants to Israel 1955-61a
15–19	0.0	0.0	0.0	0.0	0.0	0.0	0.0	0.0	0.0	0.0	0.2
20–24	0.2	0.5	0.2	0.3	0.3	0.1	0.1	0.1	0.3	0.2	0.5
25–29	1.1	1.6	1.1	1.0	1.4	0.7	0.5	1.0	1.0	0.8	1.2
30–34	2.2	2.0	2.1	1.6	2.0	1.4	1.1	1.8	1.5	1.4	1.6
35–39	2.4	2.2	2.4	1.9	2.1	1.9	1.8	2.1	1.8	1.6	1.7
40–44	2.2	2.0	2.4	2.0	1.9	2.6	2.0	3.1	1.7	1.9	1.9
45–49	2.4	1.9	2.3	2.0	1.7	2.5	1.9	3.0	1.8	2.0	1.7
50–54	2.1	1.8	2.0	2.0	1.6	2.3	1.6	3.1	n.a.	1.3	
55–59	1.8	2.0	1.9	2.2	1.4	2.6	1.7	3.8	n.a.	1.8	
60–64	1.6	2.3	1.8	2.4	1.4	2.6	1.8	3.8	n.a.	1.6	2.0
65–69	1.4	3.3	1.9	2.8	1.4	2.8	1.8	4.7	n.a.	1.7	
70+	2.2		3.0	3.4	1.8				n.a.	1.9	

Jewish Women with Virtually Completed Fertility (Aged 35–39 and Over at Enumeration), by Approximate Year When They Reached Age 25–29

Year:											
1920	2.2	3.3 {	3.0	3.2	1.8 {	2.7	2.2	4.4	n.a.	1.9 {	
1925		2.3 {		2.4	1.4				n.a.	1.7	2.0
1930	1.4	2.0	1.9	2.2	1.4 {	2.8	1.6	4.9	n.a.	1.6	
1935	1.6	1.8	1.8	2.0	1.4 }				n.a.	1.8 {	
1940	1.8	1.9	1.9	2.0	1.6	2.6	1.8	3.8	n.a.	1.3	1.7
1945	2.1	2.0	2.0	2.0	1.7	2.6	1.7	3.8	1.8	2.0	1.9
1950	2.4	2.2	2.3	1.9	1.9	2.3	1.6	3.1	1.7	1.9	1.7
1955	2.2		2.4		2.1	2.5	1.9	3.0	1.8	1.6	
1960	2.4		2.4		2.6	2.6	2.0	3.1			
1965						1.9	1.8	2.1			

aMarried women (in first marriage), by age at time of immigration.

Table XVIII   AVERAGE NUMBER OF CHILDREN

Average number of Israeli children born to woman during her
reproductive lifetime

| Period | Jewish Women born in: | | | | Moslem Women | Christian Women |
	Europe/ America	Asia/ Africa	Israel	Total		
1950–53	3.10	6.09	3.52	3.94	–	–
1965–67	2.52	4.41	2.78	3.35	9.40	4.37
1968–71	2.84	4.18	3.03	3.40	8.90	3.80
1976–77	2.89	3.54	3.00	3.10	7.51	3.23

Table XIX

Births and Deaths among Selected Jewish and General
Population in Europe, Rates per 1000 inhabitants. 1958–1977.

Place	Years	Birth rate		Death rate		Balance	
		Jewish	General	Jewish	General	Jewish	General
(1)	(2)	(3)	(4)	(5)	(6)	(7)	(8)
AUSTRIA							
Vienna	1961–65	5(a)	12	28	16	−23	−4
	1966–70	5(a)	12	28	17	−23	−5
	1971–75	7(a)	10	28	17	−21	−7
DENMARK							
Copenhagen	1960–64	12(b)	18(h)	15	10(h)	−3	+8(h)
	1965–69	14(b)	15	14	10(h)	0	+5(h)
FINLAND	1965	10(a)	17	17	10	−7	+7
FRANCE							
Paris city	1968–74	8(c)	17(i)				
Paris suburbs	1972–76	12(c)					
Belleville (Paris)	1964–68	27(e)		5		+22	
Strasbourg	1960–66	8(b)	18(i)	12	11(i)	−4	+7(i)
GERMANY, F.R.	1961–65	3(b),5(a)	18	21	11	−18,−16	+7
	1966–70	3(b),5(a)	17	20	11	−17,−15	+6
	1971–75	03(b),5(a)	11	19	12	−16,−14	−1
	1976–77	3(b)	10	19	12	−16	−2
GREAT BRITAIN	1961–65			11	12		
	1966–70	10(b)(f)	17	12	11	−2	+6
	1971–75	10(b)(g)	15	12	12	−2	+3
	1976			12	12		
Edgware (London)	1958–62	21(c)	18				
Hackney (London)	1971	13	16	16	13	−3	+3
Sheffield	1975	7(c)	16(g)	21	12(j)	−14	+4
GREECE	1964–69	7(c)	18				
ITALY	1961–65	11(b)	19	16	10	−5	+9
	1966–70	11(b)	17	15	10	−4	+7
	1971–75	10(b)	16	15	10	−5	+6
Rome	1961–65	19(b)	20	14	7	+5	+13
	1966–70	17(b)	18	12	7	+5	−11
	1971–75	16(b)	17	11	7	+5	−10

Place (1)	Years (2)	Birth rate Jewish (3)	Birth rate General (4)	Death rate Jewish (5)	Death rate General (6)	Balance Jewish (7)	Balance General (8)
Milan	1961–65	8[b]	15	12	10	−4	− 5
	1966–70	6[b]	14	12	10	−6	+ 4
	1971–75	7[b]	13	10	10	−3	+ 3
6 Medium commun.	1961–65	7[b]	13	22	10	−15	− 3
	1966–70	7[b]	14[k]	24	10[k]	−17	− 4[k]
	1971–75	5[b]	13[k]	28	10[k]	−23	+ 3[k]
15 Small commun.	1961–65	6[b]	19	22	10	−16	+ 9
	1966–70	5[b]	14[k]	18	10[k]	−13	− 4[k]
	1971–75	5[b]	13[k]	28	10[k]	−23	− 3[k]
LUXEMBOURG	1960–70	6[b]	16	15	12	− 9	+ 4
	1971–76	5[b]	12	13	12	− 8	0
NETHERLANDS	1961–65	10[c]	21				
NORWAY							
Oslo	1975	8[b]	14[n]	12	10[n]	− 4	+ 4[n]
SWEDEN							
Stockholm	1961–65	7[b]	15[l]	15	9[l]	− 8	+ 6[l]
	1966–68	3[b]	15[l]	16		− 5	+ 6[l]
	1972–76	5[b]	14[l]	19	9[l]	−14	+ 3[l]
Malmoe	1966–68	4[b]	15[l]	9	9[l]	− 5	+ 6[l]
	1972–76	9[b]	14[l]	11	11[l]	− 2	+ 3[l]
Goeteborg	1966–68	5[b]	15[l]	10	9[l]	− 5	+ 6[l]
SWITZERLAND							
	1961–65	12[a]	19	16	9	− 4	+10
	1966–70	11[a]	17	16	9	− 5	+ 8
	1971–75	12[a]	14	15	9	− 3	+ 5
	1976	13[a]	12				
Zurich	1961–65	11[d]	12	17	10	− 6	+ 2
	1966–70	12[d]	10	18	10	− 6	0
	1971–75	14[d]	9	16	11	− 2	− 2
TURKEY							
Izmir	1961–65	11[b]		14		− 3	
	1966–70	13[b]	43[m]	19	16[m]	− 6	+27[m]
	1971–75	13[b]	30[m]	20	12[m]	− 7	+27[m]

(a) Official statistics: births by religion of mother.
(b) Jewish community register.
(c) Derived from age distribution of population.
(d) Official statistics: births by religion of father.
(e) Events recorded within observed population.
(f) 1965–1969.
(g) 1971.

(h) Denmark.
(i) France.
(j) England.
(k) Italy.
(l) Sweden.
(m) Turkey.
(n) Norway.

Table XX   POPULATION OVER 55

Percentage of respective population in Israel over 55
years of age

Period	Jews	Non-Jews
1960	12.9	8.9
1970	16.7	7.5
1978	17.5	6.3

Source: Jerusalem Post, January 26, 1981 quoting from
        Society in Israel, 1980, Central Bureau of
        Statistics, Israel.

Table XXI   FERTILITY RATES PER WOMAN IN ISRAEL

Period	Jews	Non-Jews
1960	3.5	8.0
1978	2.8	6.2

Source: Ibid.

the fertility rate in the diaspora is essentially at zero or negative population growth.

A more detailed analysis of the rates in Israel demonstrates a higher, yet generally declining, fertility rate. Jewish women of European and American descent in Israel have the least number of children while Moslem women have the most; Christian Arab women have larger families than "Western Jewish" women and fewer children than do Jewish women from Arab countries.

Summarizing the demographic data of fertility rates worldwide, the following seem to be conclusions about which demographers agree: 1) Reproduction rates among heavy concentrations of Jews in urban centers conform to those of the urban population as a whole, but there is a lower rate for Jews in general. This seems to be accounted for by a combination of class and economic status, with the drive among Jews to "invest greater emotional and fiscal resources in fewer children who are thus perceived as having a physical and emotional environment that would better assure 'success;'" (75) 2) Diaspora Jews continue to differ from the majority in their country of residence by virtue of their socioeconomic stratification and where they live. This pattern is found in every country in which Jews reside. (76)

Nearly all of diaspora Jews are represented by the pattern of American Jewry, which is both "more secular, more Jewish in different subsections of the community. The American Jewish population is slowly shrinking in size, but more important, it is changing in composition, characteristics and distribution: concerns about quantitative survival nationally are much less real than the problems of the growth, size, and structure of the local Jewish communities. The future of American Jewish life is less tied to the question of whether it will survive demographically than which subsections or sections will survive." (77) Thus "an insider who knows the strengths and weaknesses of the Jewish community goes beyond the superficial indicators in trying to fathom the trends and their implications for the future." (78) This should be of greater concern to those who work within the Jewish community than the size of that community per se in the decades ahead.

SERVICES AVAILABLE: IMPLICATIONS

The preceding discussion provides the background for analysis of those issues that must engage social and communal workers throughout the Jewish world today. The present state of Jewish life in the diaspora must be evaluated in the attempt to formulate responses to issues and problems and to order the potential impact of those responses in some priority. Generally, one can categorize the kinds of services available to a family in most Jewish communities as providing, alone or in combination, one of the following: 1) physical pleasure; 2) psychological pleasure; 3) physical or psychological support or assistance; 4) defensive services; 5) services based upon commitments grounded in ideology, belief, and/or practice.

1. Physical pleasure - this category would include all programs geared to physical fitness, recreation, and/or recreationally-oriented activities where the activity itself is secondary to the enjoyment derived.

2. Psychological pleasure - this category includes activities such as discussion and personal growth: "support" groups, yoga, "self-discovery" programs, transcendental meditation programs, human potential activities, and the like.

3. Physical and or psychological support and assistance - this category encompasses many of the services now available under Jewish auspices throughout the world, and includes all manner of counseling, health services, and rehabilitation services (physical and psychological) for individuals, families, and groups.

4. Defensive services - these would encompass programs responding to real, imagined, growing, or diminished anti-Semitism, whatever its source, as well as responses to other pressures which arise from outside of the Jewish community itself, such as the need for inter-religious or inter-racial dialogue.

5. Commitment to ideology - this last category identifies the educational, cultural, religious, and Jewish content and context-oriented agencies, organizations, and institutions in Jewish life. Psychological and physical assistance services may also be subsumed in this category, insofar as they are often encompassed by general agencies which have not hesitated to help Jews under stress, regardless of age, ideology, or location.

The services provided in these categories are more actively identified with North America and are as much a function of socioeconomic and cultural levels as anything else. But to some degree they are increasingly evident throughout the world wherever Jews are found. This is especially so as Jews tend to become more hedonistic or self-serving in their lifestyles. Within Israel this changing emphasis and shift in lifestyle is more and more frequently reflected in the press.

There probably is no other voluntary community which has developed as sophisticated a response network as that of the Jews.

Yet, while the organizations which function at present respond
through the categories identified above, they may be unable to
anticipate the changing nature of the family and Jewry in general in
the decades ahead. Outside of Israel, attention to some of these
categories has been minimal due to limited resources and the limited
power of voluntary communities. Planning, the setting of priorities,
and policy making within the Jewish community outside of Israel are
all in their infancy.

In voluntary communities, membership is self-defined. The
individual Jew decides whether or not, to what degree, under what
circumstances, and within what particular time frames, he or she will
be actively involved as a Jew in organizations seen as "official"
structures, which demand active membership as measured by payment
of dues, contributions, and the like.

For increasing numbers of Jews, the matter of being Jewish is no
longer seen as a frame of reference for behaviors, but rather as a
context for feelings. There is evidence to suggest that within most
Western countries, most Jews have relatively little difficulty
identifying as Jews, but do not necessarily act upon that identification
through any overtly measurable behaviors that one could label as
being Jewish. Further, if there are behaviors which one could call
Jewish, in many instances they are private behaviors which have no
communal implications. This has a serious side effect, in that
geopolitical realities require that Jews periodically come together as
a group, both within their countries of residence and across national
borders, to help influence governments and/or other bodies to modify
actions seen as deleterious to Jewish life and/or the State of Israel.
One recent example of such communal action was the march held by
Jews in France following the Rue Copernic bombings. This protest by
tens of thousands of Jews (and other French citizens) far outweighed
hundreds of pages of written declamations on the rights of minorities
or propaganda attempting to influence the behavior of governments.

The crucial question is not whether a particular Jew or Jewish
community is trying to disappear, but rather how Jews attempt to
accommodate to the society in which they find themselves and how
they assimilate into the society, even as the society "absorbs" them
(79) As a group being pulled between the poles of universal
secularism and religious identification, Jews remain in conflict as to
how to choose between or to move to either one of these poles.
Goldscheider has talked about the theory of the collapsing middle
suggesting that the current generation has a general tendency to
move toward the pole of assimilation.

All the demographic data, particularly relating to the fourth
generation, suggest that patterns of continuity and discontinuity with

previous generations are constantly at work, with about one-third to two-fifths of the fourth generation tending toward less commitment to the Jewish community and the balance of the middle tending in the same direction. The smaller but growing "pockets of creative Jewish energy" amount to approximately one-fifth. Thus the middle has shrunk from representing about 70 percent of intensively engaged Jews in the first generation to about 40 percent in the fourth. (80) This whole process is particularly affected by the growing number of single parents, postponed marriages, and/or mixed marriages. In the context of social planning and priority setting, the problem arises of how to relate these trends and phenomena to a program of policy development and action. There is still no consensus in the Jewish community as to what responses should be developed to deal with these changing realities. For example, when one tries to deal with the problems that grow out of mixed marriages without conversion, one is immediately hindered by nonagreement as to the "appropriate" requirements for conversion.

Some agencies, especially in North America, have turned increasingly to servicing the families of mixed marriages in an attempt to be sensitively attuned to the future possibilities of conversion. This in turn has been frowned upon by some traditionally oriented Jewish communities. Very little seems to have been done officially along these lines in non-American diaspora communities, although informal discussions with social workers elsewhere suggest that there would be a desire to do so if the "organized" Jewish community would not forbid such officially sponsored attempts. (This problem of how to provide a sensitive and flexible response to questions of personal status has been brilliantly illuminated by David Ellenson in his research on Responsa literature of the nineteenth century.) (81)   One finds resistance to attempts to actively engage the homophile community within the American Jewish community, and to recruit converts to Jewish life and/or actively engage in programs of public education about Judaism for purposes of encouraging conversion among religiously unaffiliated non-Jews, as has been expressed by Rabbi Alexander Schindler and others. (82)   The European Jewish community cannot deal with some of these issues because of their own situation, which includes a lack of status and power to act as a community in their respective countries.

Voluntary communities by their nature must be based upon the desire of the self-defined members to engage in evolving strategies and acting upon those strategies. At the very least, forums for discussion, resulting in choices of action or inaction, are needed and are often not available. The achievement of a consensus for strategic action, albeit the "goal" of a voluntary community, is laden with obstacles. For example, witness the complexities involved in trying to influence or change people's attitudes about having children. On the face of it, a pro-natal policy is needed everywhere; at least to slow the downward trend in absolute numbers of births and at best to try to reverse the negative growth trend which is a reality throughout the Jewish world. As noted, of all babies born to Jews in the world, 40 percent are born in Israel, which comprises about 20 percent of the world's Jewish population. Even so, as has been noted, the natural growth patterns in Israel are themselves experiencing a downturn. The pro-natal policies which might be evolved would, of necessity, be considered differently in an autonomous Jewish state with governmental powers, than in the diaspora communities where whatever is attempted would be totally and necessarily within the context of a voluntary community. On the face of it, if any reversal in current fertility trends could be achieved, it might be assumed that only a government with its power of persuasion and taxation would be likely to effectuate such a change.

Such was the consideration of Dr. Roberto Bachi, the world's foremost Jewish demographer, who, as early as the 1930s, concluded that the fertility rate of Jews would prove to be the overriding demographic Jewish concern once a Jewish state was established. In the 1930s, he saw the descending trend lines and understood that even though the birthrates were not yet below the reproduction rate, fertility rates were rapidly dropping among Jews. He urged David Ben-Gurion to regard the Jewish birthrate as a matter of high priority in Israeli government social policy planning. (83) His private discussions and public writings continued to sound the bell of concern and as the enormity of Hitler's "accomplishments" came to be known, the long-range implications of Bachi's dire warnings were increasingly appreciated by Ben-Gurion. Accordingly, after the establishment of the State of Israel, one of the first acts of the Knesset was to introduce a series of incentives to encourage larger families. In addition to the introduction of cash payments for each child, special prizes and awards to large families were made. The economic importance of these allowances was not inconsiderable, for as recently as 1974 the cash allowance represented nine percent of the average monthly salary of a three-child family, 30 percent of a six-child family, and 50 percent of a nine-child family. (84) Israel's provisions were unique, for these policies were instituted at a time of high immigration, even though pro-natal policies have historically "almost always [been] related to periods of low immigration." (85)

The cash gifts and prizes offered by the government in the early days of the state were quietly abolished after a few years because it was found that Arab women were consistently the prize winners. (86) Still later, the awards were reestablished under Jewish Agency auspices so they could be granted solely to Jews through other than government sources. As it was discovered that there was no appreciable effect upon the downward trend of birth rates, the prizes were quietly abolished in the late 1950s. (87) However, the system of family allowance is still in effect in Israel.

Israel has continued to focus on high fertility rates as the single most important factor for Jewish survival and continuity. This focus has been at a much higher degree of consciousness and consistency among Israeli opinion makers than has been the case in the diaspora communities. The implications of the continued downward trend in the birthrate has greatest dramatic implications in Israel, with even broader and graver consequences for Israel-diaspora relations than heretofore appreciated. Yet, any discussion about the quality of life in general and Jewish family life in particular is ultimately and inevitably related to the intersection of two sets of data: How many children are being born and who is giving birth to the children?

The data reviewed clearly demonstrate a consistent pattern in the diaspora. That pattern encompasses an increasingly affluent, consistently urban, highly educated, increasingly mobile, Westernized, and secularized Jewish population. These Jews are aging; barely, if at all, reproducing themselves; less likely to affiliate formally with Jewish organizations if they are under the age of 35; often postponing marriage and parenting; and, in general, tending to more idiosyncratic and individualistic behavior patterns when responding to what is generally viewed as normative, responsible behavior. This description does not encompass the traditionally oriented Jewish community which, though still small, seems to be growing both numerically and in the intensity of commitment to its goals. (88)

PROBLEMS IN ISRAEL

The concerns which Bachi voiced to Ben-Gurion had several unforeseen ramifications. In addition to demographic implications, it has been shown that the people most concerned with the quality of family life in Israel (as in the West in general) have the lowest number of children and the highest number of abortions. Although Jews have traditionally had an ambivalent attitude toward abortion, over one-third of urban Jewish women in Israel married 25 years or more had at least one abortion, while 49 percent of all Israeli-born women had at least one abortion in the same period. (89)

The trend toward an increasingly aging Jewish population, both in Israel and the diaspora, partly as a result of smaller family size, means that fewer adults will be available to give support to the aged. In the decade ahead, it is estimated that there will be a decline of one-third in the number of potential breadwinners able to support the elderly. (90)

This trend has particularly important ramifications in Israel when one realizes that over the next 20 years these demographic changes will produce an increasing social gap between the Jews of Oriental origin (the edot hamizrah) and the Jews from the West or of European origin (Ashkenazim). Because the edot hamizrah have tended to have larger families, an irreversible trend has been set in motion for the next two decades. Fewer children can continue their education, for their income is needed by the family. In contrast to diaspora Jewry, a markedly smaller percentage of all Israelis attain high levels of secular education and this is especially true of the children of the edot hamizrah. As noted, presently 80 percent of working adults in Israel are in white collar, professional, managerial, or business occupations. By the year 2000 this figure will be down to 57 percent as a result of a number of factors, including a "combination of a growing aged sector of the population, the shift in socioeconomic and ethnic composition of the aged (and the population as a whole) and the traditional dependence of the aged on family support. This will accentuate a host of welfare and institutional problems early in the twenty-first century." (91)

This was not the intended outcome of the recommendations made by international leaders to the State of Israel in the mid-1960s. These recommendations included a strong public propaganda program encouraging a higher birthrate among Jews; the dissemination of information on birth control and family planning; the adjusting of employment conditions to encourage working women to have more children by giving them paid maternity leave, special tax allowances, and educational credits; providing increased government assistance to large families; attempting to reduce the number of abortions by allowing them to be carried out legally in public hospitals; and establishing a special demographic center. (92) In reality, these policies did little to change the trends, for "Israeli families, as those in other societies, do not reproduce for the 'benefit of the nation' even if the nation provides some assistance." (93)

At present, experts disagree with regard to the demographic impact of "pro-natal" policies in Israel. Despite the anxiety about the trend to zero population growth, the "fallout" from mixed marriages, and the fact that 40 percent of all Jewish babies are being born in Israel, some demographers have predicted a worldwide Jewish population as high as 17.5 million by 1990 and 21.8 million by 2010. Although the population figures in some countries will drop precipitously, the existence of Israel as a source of growth and North America as a predictable base for relative stability lead to these projections. (Very little variance is expected as a result of policies within Israel for "even the most effective pro-natal policies in Israel contribute marginally to the size and growth rate of the population of the world.") (94) These population projections -- of 17.5 million and 21.8 million respectively -- contradict projections by other demographers, such as Bergman, who predict the possibility of as few as 900,000 Jews worldwide in the next century. (95)

What other factors must be examined in order to evaluate these contradictory demographic projections? Certainly one central factor is the impact of the culture of the larger society on the individual family. Among other factors, American culture may be described and evaluated by observing how people spend their time, income, wealth, and resources; what they define as their needs; how they behave in daily life; who and what they honor, value, and revere; and how the nation expresses these preferences and choices through public and government expenditures, priorities, and concerns.

VI

VALUES IN WESTERN SOCIETY

There is no doubt that contemporary Jews have been shaped to a definitive extent by Western society. The ability of the Jews as a polity to respond, or more importantly, to anticipate and shape strategies which will modify the resulting profile is limited by a number of realities. The Jews in Eastern Europe have minimal community structures and are able to do little to influence or change their current lifestyles, let alone evolve strategies for intensifying Jewish life and/or moderating tendencies toward assimilation. Indeed, unless the governmental policies of the Eastern European bloc change radically there is little likelihood that 50 years hence Jews, as we know them, will be present there in any discernible form as a vital or even identifiable Jewish community. The ramifications of these realities, in relation to the problem of Jewish identity, can only be understood in the context of the sources of commitment. This inevitably leads to an examination of peoples' values as a source for their commitments vis-a-vis their identity as Jews.

DEFINING VALUES

Charles Morris has pointed out that "the term 'value' is one of the great words, and, like other such words ('science,' 'religion,' 'art,' 'morality,' 'philosophy') its meaning is multiple and complex." At times it refers to "tendencies or disposition of living things to prefer one kind of object rather than another. Such values may be called operative values." Another use of the term may imply "preference for a symbolically indicated object" - thus differentiating it from the operative sphere. Sometimes, he continues, the term is "concerned with what is preferable or 'desirable' regardless of whether it is in fact preferred or conceived as preferable." We sometimes call something important even though we are not prepared to act as if it is. In each instance, the word "value" involves the element of preference. He concludes that "preferential behavior" should define the value field. (96)

Wheelis emphasizes the general character of values. "Those things which men do, prize, and hold dear are termed values - without reference to their validity. Where effort and devotion and allegiance are committed, there value resides for those who so commit their energies." (97) Pumphrey has stated that "values are abstract formulations or prescriptions for preferred behavior held in common by social groups, and having emotional meaning for members of the group. They imply a customary preference for certain means, ends, and conditions of life." (98)

Most social psychologists hold that over and above individual values there exist social values which "form the major (directive) part" of the personality. (99) These are concepts which originate in and direct the behavior of groups and are thus seen as "consequently important conceptions (standards) of desirability which influence behavior and to which conduct is referred for judgment of goodness, appropriateness, and the like." (100)

Samuel Kohs has properly reminded us that the "conscious modeling of a social order with values appropriate for both conformity and diversity is far from a simple task. We are not satisfied with what we have, and we are not sure what we want or need." (101)

Since time immemorial, the goal of groups of individuals with shared value systems has been to infuse social institutions with their values in the hope that the society at large would become harmonious with their ideas and aspirations. Implicit in the process of affecting societal change, whether through imposition or exposure, has been the assumption that the ultimate measure of a value is the resultant modification of behavior. Thus, in addition to prizing or cherishing that which we choose, we affirm the choice by acting differently as a result, and we repeat our acts as a measure of the impact the value has upon us. (102)

In truth, there are few universally accepted values. In reality, contending forces within and between societies have historically tended to vie for power and position overtly and covertly, seeking to impose their value system on the society at large. Groups which are successful in this effort achieve approval for their values that is clearly stated and understood. Actions or behaviors by the members of the group congruent with these values will then be more likely to occur. In general, priorities for action flow from the values deemed most important by the specific group.

At present Western society is confronted with a choice between two essentially disparate value systems. Each of these systems is partially rooted in Judaism and Christianity, with uneven mixtures of positivism, rationalism, hedonism, and existentialism. Within these value systems are manifest differences in attitudes about the nature of humans and their world.

In Western society we tend to glorify things at the expense of people. Underlying this attitude is the presupposition that things - property - are worthy of more care and consideration than people.

Property rights and human rights have historically contended for primary concern since human beings began to live in social groups. In the Western world today there is every evidence to suggest that the right of property ownership supersedes other social considerations.

Action "hallmarks" of those espousing this philosophy in the United States often include those who oppose environmental protection laws, right to work laws, and zoning. However, a stance supporting specific social or political policies such as zoning laws and environmental controls does not automatically imply fundamental human concern. A value system which includes caring about people, when joined with concern for the environment, as well as property, attempts to strike a delicate balance between sometimes antithetical poles. A concern for social betterment through intelligent use of land, energy, and human talents emerges from a sense of interdependence between humans and their environment. The simplistic approaches of some who are in vanguard of resistance to social change bring their own perils in turn.

THE AMERICAN VALUE BASE

Underlying much of the American value system are variations of Calvinistic doctrines of rugged individualism and pre-destination. Ambivalent attitudes toward the human condition, the nature of people and their perfectibility (or lack thereof), and positive attitudes toward materialism, unbridled capitalism, and individualism were dominant in the United States in its formative pioneering period. The tension resulting from this ambivalence was often expressed in self-fulfilling prophecies offered to explain the success of the "winners" and the low place of the "losers." God's will prevailed, no matter what the realities of the social conditions.

This puritanism and the frontier attitude were often in direct conflict. Successive waves of immigrants vied in their haste to integrate into the larger society and take on the outward characteristics of the dominant culture, perceived as White Anglo-Saxon Protestantism. Parallel to the American Calvinist-based individualistic "pessimism," there existed another view of life in the United States, drawn from nineteenth century European rational optimism. People were seen as perfectible and society defined as a community of concerned and responsible interrelating groups and individuals.

Most American Jewish organizations, begun in the nineteenth and early twentieth centuries, were founded by those who shared these attitudes. From the beginning to the middle of the twentieth century, this optimistic world view was in the ascendancy. America's inhabitants were seen as the new chosen people. In one important regard these thinkers departed from the Jewish role of the last two millennia and remained authentic to Christian doctrine. The Good News had to be shared with the world - thus came the period of "Americanizing" the world, with Jews often in the vanguard. The rest is history. The point to be concluded, however, is prologue to the future. Americans have not accepted the dominant values of those who led and lead such groups. Attitudes and values in American life strain for re-definition and new application.

The dominant outlook still prevalent in the government and among the majority of America's institutions suggests that people are not to be trusted, that equality is a myth, that profits supersede social responsibility, and that the Earth is not the Lord's. Thus, by examining the real policies of institutions as they function, and ignoring their rhetoric, we find a materialistic, individualistic, suspicious, fear-ridden, and hedonistic society, encouraged in these characteristics by its national (and local) government. We see that in reality there is a great gap between the value systems espoused by the U.S. society and given lip service by individuals, and we recognize the gap between the value systems and the actions taken by organizations and individuals.

There was an arrogance at the core of nineteenth and twentieth century utopian liberal thinking. Its unstated but implicit image of the future was a projection of an over-simplified, monolithic, and "homogenized" approach for the solving of problems and the setting of goals to achieve desired lifestyles. With something bordering on fanatic zeal, liberal middle class people, who comprise the mainstay of American middle class organizations, set out to save America and the world from its problems and divisiveness. In their blithe and naive ignorance, they lost sight of the reality that the maintenance of certain individual and group differences is at the heart of a healthy society.

The issue of busing as a tool for racial and social integration might be considered as a classic case in point. Underlying the support for busing is the presumption that integration is good and segregation is bad. It is further assumed that education under segregated conditions is bad while under integrated conditions it is good. The federal and state court decisions of the 1950s gave impetus and support to these assumptions. Much of society's efforts to these ends were initially focused upon the South, where the issue was first brought to the attention of the courts.

However, the 1970s saw different responses to the issue of busing as compared to the mood of the 1950s. Busing came North. Black aspirations and self-perceptions were quite different from before;

ethnic enclaves had been created which were now being threatened. Questions were raised about the validity of the value assumptions, suggesting that prejudice is reinforced and educational attainment lowered as a result of indiscriminate use of integration. "Liberalism," in the face of ethnicity, was insulting.

ETHNICITY

During this time, Western society witnessed a growth in the valuing of ethnicity - a sense of group self. Jews can be grateful to other ethnic minorities for having made group differences as "kosher" as individual differences and, indeed, the legitimacy of group differences remains salient for all today. Groups shape ideals, as well as families, values, and behaviors. A pride in group "self" can and should lead to a pride in self and ultimately result in a better coping, functioning, and responsible human being. Kurt Lewin was the first to raise this concept to something approaching a scientific postulate when he did his then radical studies in small group theory at the University of Iowa in the 1940s.

In addition to ethnicity, during the past two decades a trend toward "Me-ism" (Tom Wolfe's felicitous phrase) has become manifest. Segments of American and Western society began to focus on the individual and not the group. Thus, while ethnic identification was increasingly valued by all ethnic groups, the values and demands that a particular group expected or needed from its "natural" members were simultaneously modified and minimized.

As has been stated, people often find in group self-identification the security of knowing that they are indeed worthwhile individuals as members of ethnic groups legitimately accepted by the larger society. There is, however, a risk that they might misuse that self-identification as a rationale for turning from broader issues which must continue to involve every member of society. Stein and Hill have cautioned us on the limits of ethnicity in referring to one's ethnic background "[that] what was once a badge of shame...has now become not merely a source of pride but often a weapon of haughtiness. In the United States nowadays everything but WASP is beautiful." (103) They warn that too strong a group identification can lead to xenophobia; in turning inward to their own groups exclusively for self-affirmation, people may reject the "moral imperative" of common concerns and fall victim to egoism and short-sightedness.

On the other hand, research has demonstrated that a lack of sustaining traditions often becomes a context for social and individual crisis. The need for community may be the individual's decisive need, and its absence may explain the existence and exacerbation of anomie and alienation, the "curse" of the modern era. There is a great deal of evidence suggesting that "cultural, ethnic, religious, and...political traditions contribute importantly to ego identity and integrity." (104) Fingaretta said it well: "The essence of anxiety is the experience of meaning less." (105) For many, if not most people, the ethnic group has been a central source of meaning, even though it is not the sole framework for identity formation. Eagle has compiled a considerable body of evidence to indicate that the access to tradition which the group provides, coupled with belief and attachment, has a profound effect upon individuals: "Adults living alone, with few or no attachments to family, kin or other groups are more susceptible to tuberculosis, multiple accidents, alcoholism, schizophrenia and suicide." (106) Bettelheim and Frankl have emphasized that attachments to people, ideals, and an idea of the future resulted in higher survival rates in concentration camps and among prisoners of war than was the case in those lacking these attachments. (107)

The influence of ethnic groups is also linked to size and compresence. Living in ethnic communities produces outcomes impossible to achieve in heterogeneous settings. Rabbin and Struening have pointed out that "as a given ethnic group constitutes a smaller proportion of the total in a particular area, diagnosed rates of mental illness increase both in comparison to the rates for other ethnic groups in that area and to members in the same ethnic group in neighborhoods where they constitute a significant proportion or majority." (108) This same finding has been confirmed in research among Chinese in Canada, (109) the French and English-speaking groups in Quebec, (110) and the black and white residents in various census tracts in Baltimore. (111)

The following conclusions may be drawn: 1) To be "real," values must be demonstrable in behaviors; 2) so-called traditional values which once had components of social concern and responsibility are no longer the dominant values of most Americans because they have become so individualistic; and yet 3) research indicates that identification with one's ethnicity and ethnic group, when capitalized upon as a source of nourishment, is a source of values, stability and better mental health.

THE JEWISH RESPONSE

Fusion of family and community institutions must be effectuated. Alliances must be encouraged which will have the greatest chance of helping families to shape and live out their values in the home and in their communities. Institutions must combine forces without losing their respective and unique identities. Their goal must be to counter the value orientation represented in the "Me-istic" and self-centered outlooks. The Wall Street Journal, 21 January 1982, reported results of a study by Doyle, Dane, and Bernbach that a substantial and increasing percentage of middle aged people, while agreeing on the importance of the family, were "less and less willing to sacrifice for it." They were 'living in the present' and worrying less about the future; feeling that their children will have to get along with less from them. (112) Ironically, a study by Yankelovich indicated that young people felt less inclined to be concerned about taking care of their parents because they did not see them as prime responsibility. (113)

The implications of such data make it clear that Jewish community leaders cannot indulge in platitudes in dealing with these matters. Social science research demonstrates that there must be a balance of individual good and community responsibility with community good and individual responsibility, in order for both society and individual to be "healthy" and successful.

VII

BACKGROUND

Defining Jewish Life

All that has happened to Jews in the past and all that is happening to Jews today shapes the definition of what is Jewish. Historical events, theological perceptions, legal prescriptions and proscriptions, contemporary realities -- all impinge upon and influence the psyche and very being of the Jew today, <u>even as every Jew always and everywhere has been influenced</u>, negatively or positively, by these phenomena.

One example of this complex process may suffice. The nineteenth century "enlightened" Jew in Germany who decided to convert to Christianity was responding to his Jewish condition with what he deemed positive behavior. Other Jews of the time evolved radical new Jewish forms of identification (literally, "reforms"), alongside still other Jews who simply ignored being Jewish in order to escape the negative effects of the newly open society. All three responses reflected what was regarded by each Jew as appropriate behavior, although each behavior had a different effect upon the individual Jew, the Jewish community, and the future.

What Jews experience may be viewed negatively or positively depending upon the perspective of the time, the person, and the impact of that experience upon Jews as a people. The Holocaust was a horrendously negative experience for the Jewish people. However, conclusions drawn from this experience by the survivors themselves were highly variable. Some survivors renewed their lives as Jews with a fervor which bespoke their thanks to God for having been able to live through such unspeakable horror. For others the giving of testimony against man's bestiality was and is seen as an opportunity to serve God in ever more pietistic, realistic, traditional terms. Others argued that Jews throughout the ages have been persecuted for being "different" and as a result, some had tried to become like everyone else, i.e. to assimilate, as many did in Germany; Hitler was believed to have punished the grandchildren of the assimilated Jews because they had become too much like the Germans and in the process had "diluted" the "purity" of the "master race." Thus, this group of Jews asserted, we had been damned for being too different from others and then damned for being the same as others. Perhaps we should continue to be Jews regardless of what the non-Jewish world says or feels about us. Yet others concluded that the

Holocaust came upon the Jews because they had not succeeded in vanishing from Europe. This group has tended to choose total assimilation - removing itself from Jewish life, changing names and sometimes even other physical appearance, and moving to places distant from other Jews, all in the hope of sparing themselves and their progeny the pain of being labeled Jewish.

What Jews believed and believe shapes the least religious among us even as it guides the most devout. A Jewish atheist does not really merit that label unless, as Hillel taught, he understands what he denies. However, to define being a Jew only in theological terms does a great disservice to the historical and legal (halachic) definitions of Judaism, which define a Jew by birth and not by belief. Definition based on belief is an inaccurate criterion which has led people, especially contemporary youth, to a false syllogism: "Judaism is a religion; I am not religious; therefore, I am not a Jew." The Drew study of college freshmen in the early part of this decade found 17 percent of the Jewish respondents stating that their parents were Jews, but that they themselves were not, because they did not believe in God.

For some an ideological belief system has replaced or superseded the theological. A generation of Marxist-inspired socialist-Zionists has successfully fused a modern political/ social secularist ideology with an ancient dream and profoundly identified themselves as Jews, even as the name of God was hardly relevant to their Jewish practices. Nonetheless, in studying the Bible, even these secularist Jews perceive that whether or not God exists, the Jews of ancient (and many of recent) times lived as if He did. That belief (however misplaced) has produced, if not a "God-intoxicated" people, a "good-intoxicated" people.

For other Jews, confrontation with the reality of Jewish history has led to a Zionist ideology, encompassing messianic and universalistic overtones shared by the most traditional among us. They espouse the ideology of achieving "normalcy" in Israel - the hope that Jews there will be like people everywhere else - but they also stand side by side with Jews who pray fervently for the messianic period when all people shall be as one in preparation for the acceptance of the One God.

There are yet others for whom the "cultural" or "folk" components of Jewish life substitute for matters of theology or ideology in defining and expressing their identity. Jewish artifacts, stories, legends, languages, music, food, and perhaps most important of all, kinship ties (although almost all of these folk elements reflect influences and transmutations from other peoples in whose midst Jews have dwelled) provide comfort, nourishment, familiarity, and a framework for Jewish life. In its most attenuated form, the eating of lox, bagels, and cream cheese on Sunday mornings in America may be, for some Jews, nearly the last remnant of their cultural heritage. The sense of cultural identity can also manifest itself through hearing Schoenberg's opera "Moses and Aaron" or Bernstein's "Jeremiah Symphony," looking at a painting by Chagall, or reading a story by Kafka or a poem by Karl Shapiro. Benjamin Disraeli's identification with his Jewish ancestors, despite his conversion to Christianity, exemplifies some of the ironies, contradictions, and inconsistencies found in the varying manifestations of "Jewish identity."

Many people seek (and find) psychological comfort in being Jews and engage in Jewish practices not out of obedience to or belief in a divine imperative, but out of a need for psychological ease. They _feel_ good to be Jewish and do "Jewish things" with fellow Jews, be it on the golf course or in the theater lobby. These American Jews can be described more often than not as discreetly identifiable groups of ethnically "homogenized" people. They find comfort in engaging in shared activities which are a function of their own socioeconomic position and are best enjoyed with other people like themselves of similar socioeconomic and ethnic background.

Most Jews today would deny adherence to theological imperatives even as they select from the 613 commandments in Jewish tradition those which comfort them or which they find most satisfying. The recent upsurge in Jewish practice on a personal and communal level grows out of a search for adjustment rather than a return to a belief in God.

The contemporary American situation encourages these phenomena. Ethnicity is at its height; group membership has been labeled socially acceptable and desirable by many highly respected authority figures including political figures and movie heroes. Within the group called Jews, the externally marginal people receive emotional and psychological support. Sometimes anomalies result wherein the group is expected or expects to act publicly in a manner which is at variance with individual behavior: Jews who eat non-kosher foods in restaurants or at home may demand that only kosher food be served at public Jewish functions. Concomitantly, the public actions of Jews might also emerge from what they feel or perceive the general community to think or do vis-a-vis their behavior. The question "What will the gentiles say?" has ebbed and flowed throughout history as a sometime guide for public Jewish behavior.

The geopolitical realities are no less important a factor influencing Jewish practice. Washington watches the level of

American Jewish donations to Jewish "causes" as one way to assess the degree of unity or the appearance of discord or apathy on the part of American Jewry. Perhaps Israel's response to diaspora Jewry as a sometimes full and always present partner to life in Israel may then be seen as an expression of the harsh realities of political clout and "trade-offs"? How can 2.6 percent of the U.S. population maintain a relationship with a Congress and an administration which will result in a sympathetic response to "Jewish" requests and at the same time feel free to criticize the administration when the legitimate interests of non-Jews are being ignored or subverted? Does anyone truly believe anything could be done to help Israel, or Jews here or elsewhere, if coalitions were not continually being formed and understandings negotiated and reached with all manner of other groups on the American scene? It is doubtful whether ethnic groups of lower socioeconomic status will tolerate paying high prices for gas in America when Israel gets fuel guaranteed by the U.S. government, unless Jews agree to reciprocate by helping other ethnic groups with their economic and political concerns.

A "Jewish" Jewish family brings these concerns to its table and thus reads, watches, listens and talks with a sense that separates and screens. The Jewish family is thus the place for possibility and pain; promise and hope where the global is sifted and dealt with in the most personal of ways. How did this happen in the past? Will it happen in the future?

THE SECRET OF THE JEWS

Historically, Judaism was able to strike a balance between individual good and community responsibility and community good and individual responsibility. This balance was achieved through continuing celebrations which themselves were concerned with the balance between the person and community; and with both individual/particular and universal/communal values. By defining expectations through rituals, which in turn evoke memories of the creation of those expectations, and by demanding responses -- both individual and communal -- rabbinic genius wove the tapestry called Jewish living.

It is my premise that the following elements represent a replicable model for Jews today and for all other groups who seek to build value-laden communities. The Jews wove eight strands to build their community. Not all contemporary Jews live within their context; the most consistently committed do. Each strand is open to flexible interpretation and modification based on consensus within broad parameters. Their resulting varying applications by Jews resulted in the phenomena that we call Jewish and Judaism today. They are: 1) memories, 2) behaviors, 3) a sense of interdependence and responsibility, 4) a sense of a common or shared fate, 5) encompassment of a belief system, 6) foundation of knowledge, 7) optimism, 8) assumption of a future.

1. Memories

Informed Jewish families and communities re-enact, through structured and time-framed ritual, a wide range of historical events which have befallen the Jewish people. They are not all sad in nature. Indeed, one is commanded in the observance of the Purim holiday to become so inebriated as to be unable to distinguish between an arch villain and a prototypical hero. Each Sabbath, we joyously partake in blessing and drinking wine, in awesome remembrance of the beginnings of the very universe. The most widely celebrated holiday, Passover, remembers the bitterness of slavery in the context of a celebration of freedom and responsibility.

2. Behaviors

Out of these memories grow and continue to grow behaviors, some ancient, some new, some individualized and many communal, but all trying to codify uniqueness, ethical values, heroes and/ or events of great and small moment to the world and of abiding importance to Jews.

Thus, the subtle action of the traditional housewife in removing knives from the table at the end of the Sabbath dinner is done quietly to remind all who thank God for the meal just completed that even symbolic instruments of war should not be present when thanking God for sustenance gained. And the blessing after a meal is recited to remind the human being who finds it so easy to petition God in advance for sustenance (however understood) to remain thankful after gratification.

3. Sense of Interdependence

There are many kinds of Jews and many ways to be a Jew in both individual and collective terms. Historically, the collectivity was more dominant. Modernity has defined the Jewish community as a voluntary collectivity. Corporate disabilities are not suffered by the Jew in America -- nor are there compulsory obligations. There are 613 commandments in the Bible. While they are not listed in a hierarchical way, for the modern Jew, the one which remains observed consciously and assiduously by more Jews than any

other (excepting, more or less, the ten commandments) is Tzedakah --
responsible and required giving to help others. While weakening among
the younger generations as the Jews become more "Americanized,"
this sense of interdependence and common concern continues to
manifest itself in not only the giving of money, but in the giving of
time and energy. There is an active Jewish "lobby" on the American
Jewish scene. Communal concern is manifest also in the existence of
hundreds of organizations operating openly to help Jews in need
throughout the world.

4. Sense of Common Fate

The sense of interdependence, when it exists, is triggered
and reinforced by memories and expected behaviors. The inter-
interaction reminds Jews that what befalls one Jew affects another.
As a rootless people which defied history by retaining a self without
a land - the only community to do so successfully for so long a
period - the Jews are aware of the ever present possibility of their
fortunes changing rapidly in the world at large. The Jews have been
called the "ever-dying people." This bitter awareness, in turn, has
resulted in teachings which inform in a different way than others
operative today. We are, for example, in a society where caveat
emptor - let the buyer beware - is a dominant value. However, the
Jew was taught historically to let the seller beware, for it is
incumbent upon the seller to assure fair weights and measures,
appropriate goods for fair value and vice versa. If one Jew cheated,
the community felt responsible. The sense of common fate per-
meates Jews of all manner and means. If we are to die, it is not
to be because we gave up our values, but because we are
commanded to live by our beliefs.

5. A Belief System

This "God-intoxicated people," as Revan has called the Jews,
attend religious services less frequently than any group in
America, profess to believe in God less than is the case with
other groups, and yet continue to have a higher sense of concern
with moral and social justice when compared to other groups.

While these anomalies exist, the family and the community
institutions actuate, at their best, the belief in imitatio deo,
even if the theological explications leave Jews uncomfortable.
The belief is in the capacity of the human being to be God-like
by acting "good," even as this expectation, rooted as it is in
some transcendental frame of reference, presents the children of
God, the Jewish people, with a problem in relating to their
Parent.

6. Knowledge

The People of the Book are at times accused of having become the People of the buck. If the success story of the Jew in America is to be understood, the power of the myth of learnedness must be fully appreciated. I say myth because there is enough evidence to suggest that not all Jews were, or are, learned. A surprising number of Jews who immigrated to America in the late nineteenth and early twentieth century were illiterate. And yet there is no question that a commitment to education has been a relatively consistent value and behavior. Compulsory education, for example, was first established by the Jews 2,000 years ago, and even today Jews worldwide are among the highest educated wherever they reside.

7. Optimism

Grounded in the realities of oppression, abject poverty, defeats, dispersions, discrimination, and death, the Jewish people remained and remain remarkably optimistic. Humor sustained and sustains even as the prophetic diatribes always end in the context of possible redemption. Literature and folk wisdom abound with this continuing sense of "the possible." Whether faced with the possibility of a new world flood without the benefit of a Noah and vowing to learn to breathe underwater, or putting on plays and organizing symphony orchestras in the death camps, there has been this faith. Not that there has not been ques- tioning. For the tradition has it that on more than one occasion God Himself has been put on trial for His mistreatment of His people; to the point that one great rabbi was known to have asked God to give the Jews a rest and "choose" some other people for a change, if to be chosen was exemplified by the experiences they had undergone as a result of their chosenness.

8. Future Oriented

Hartman has written of joy and responsibility as the hall-marks of the Jewish people. He has eloquently spoken of these capacities as potentialities for renewing the Jews and the world. All of Jewish history is predicated on a tomorrow, grounded in opti-mistic fulfillment. Whether in anticipation of the Messiah or the messianic age, where peace and tranquility would abide in abundance and perpetuity, the sense of future has been shaped and reshaped in the Jewish reality.

One Hassidic sect spends considerable effort in asking Jewish adult males to don phylacteries because they believe that if every Jewish male over the age of 13 was to perform this mitzva (imperative act) just once, the Messiah would promptly appear the following Sabbath. And most importantly, precisely because every Jewish male did not perform this act yesterday, the Hassidim must return tomorrow to continue to help "pave the way" for the Messiah in the future. Indeed, one Jewish leader teaches that one most pray to God for the appearance of the Messiah, and to act God-like in case he does not arrive.

In sum, the strands are transferable and utilizable - not by individuals alone or schools or religious institutions alone; not by an amorphous society or by government alone; but by thoughtful reciprocal acts reflected in literature, humor, art, drama, family patterns and celebrations. Most importantly all are grounded in a sense of community. For the Jew outside of a community cannot sustain Jewish life and living. This partnership with and within the Jewish family at its "best" is the refractor for the prisms shining out of the past.

VIII

CHALLENGES AND STRATEGIES

Working with Jews in the Decades Ahead

The task of the Jewish community in upbuilding the family is to discern when specific conflicts/problems become legitimate community concerns. It is far easier to obtain a consensus on issues relevant to Jews as a group than on issues which are traditionally personal and private in nature. Thus, it would be the rare community of Jews not immediately ready to petition the government for aid to Israel when Israel's physical safety is at risk. If Israel's safety can be seen as an area of broad consensus, one can compare the nature and extent of Jewish concerns to a large sieve with increasingly finely meshed screens through which the issues must be sifted. As the sifting process continues, the disagreement on or the Jewish response to issues increases. For example, while almost all Jews in America favor Jewish action in America on behalf of Israel's survival, the Jewish community does not agree on how the West Bank problem should be solved.

On the local level, issues become increasingly complex as they focus on matters of seemingly personal and private concern. One instance is the planning of Saturday programs in Jewish community centers in ways that are "consonant with the spirit of the Sabbath." Bitter discussions ensued when a particular community center implemented the principle with specific programs while simultaneously attempting to placate both its Orthodox and secular members.

Within Israel, the definition, modification, and implementation of social policies are the day-to-day business of the government, the Jewish Agency, the Joint Distribution Committee, and countless private and semiprivate entities. The balance of this essay will focus on an agenda for the North American Jewish community which is developing a voluntaristic polity within which social policy concerns can be evolved, identified, and to limited degrees, acted upon. (114) They form the context within which families will grow, be developed and served.

Woocher, following Elazar, posits seven principles which guide the American Jewish community (which is to be viewed increasingly as a political system or polity that is an entity evolving some governance mechanisms). He suggests that within the American Jewish community there is a kind of "institution" which encompasses intersecting principles:

73

1) <u>voluntarism</u>: that citizenship in the polity is a matter of choice;

2) <u>associationalism</u>: that the basis of the polity is the coming together of Jews in association for a variety of self-selected purposes;

3) <u>federalism</u>: that the relationships between and among the associations comprising the polity are by and large confederal or federal, i.e., nonhierarchical and noncentralized in character, and that power is widely distributed among the associations;

4) <u>republicanism</u>: that the polity is ultimately responsible to (and sovereignty ultimately resides in) the Jewish public as a whole, and not in any single group or individual;

5) <u>consensualism</u>: that decisions should reflect the agreement of a substantial portion of the active citizenry;

6) <u>active self-defense</u>: that Jewish associations should protect the rights of Jews and seek to combat anti-Semitism; and

7) <u>mutual responsibility</u>: to provide for the needs of other Jews. (115)

The key to evolving appropriate social policy strategies is an understanding of the system in which they will be used. The voluntary nature of Jewish life in America is predicated upon a political system interacting with what Elazar calls participating publics. (116) Unfortunately, as he points out, we are confronted with an increasingly energetic core elite dealing with an increasingly passive Jewish population. Social policy concerns or priorities must therefore be viewed as 1) primarily educative in their usefulness and/or, 2) forming the basis for action within the associations of Jewish life which are energized and nourished by, and give guidance to, the Jewish "elite" and/or other Jewishly committed individuals.

FOCUS ON THE FAMILY

In America there has now emerged a general consensus as to the primacy of the family as the main issue for concern. There is hardly an agency or organization on the local and national level which has not issued a <u>pronunciamento</u> on the need to do "something" to help the Jewish family. The phase of so-called "needs assessment" is at its height and, ironically, is probably reaching a peak of sophistication at the moment that the resources available to the Jewish community appear to be at their nadir. The need for arriving at consensus is not obviated by this reality but rather intensifies the need to re-ratify the community agenda so that the polity may respond in ways appropriate to its capacities and its functions. Given the approach toward consensus the specific strategies may be undertaken singly and/or jointly, depending upon circumstances and urgency of needs.

Among the many organizations which have dedicated increasing time and money to the needs of the Jewish family are the American Jewish Committee, the Jewish Welfare Board, and the Council of Jewish Federations. Each has highlighted services to the family as a social policy issue of the highest priority and has published materials to help develop strategies in local communities which will strengthen Jewish family life. (117)

In her monograph for the American Jewish Committee, Kamerman's strategies are mostly predicated upon the Jewish community's forming coalitions. She identifies three strategies which have great implications for all of America, including the Jewish community. They are demand side social policy, public-private partnerships and corporate social welfare. (118) These are strategies viewed not as substitutes for government action (with which she urges the Jewish community to associate itself) but as alternatives, either as substitutes or supplements, as appropriate.

Demand side social policy achieves social goals by providing subsidies through tax credits or vouchers enabling consumers to purchase essential services in the marketplace. (119) The premise (not necessarily hers) is that this approach is a counter to supply side economics and could aid in the dismantling of burgeoning bureaucracies. It could also have untoward consequences by lowering the quality of services available. Voucher systems thus developed could conceivably increase competition and encourage individual choice but could modify existing social service delivery systems in the process.

Public-private partnerships presume the limitations of a free market approach and encourage shared initiative between the private sectors. Among the problems to be guarded against are lack of clarity regarding accountability and rigidity in bureaucracies, public or private. (120)

Corporate social welfare refers to the increasing support given to families through extended fringe benefits to employees. These have direct economic impact upon families to a negative or positive degree, depending upon the extent of the fringe benefits which today can amount to up to 37 percent of payroll costs. (121)

Now for the basic question. Can a voluntarily-based community adapt a series of objectives and strategies which 1) will penetrate the institutions which serve Jews and; 2) will enable them to learn from models developed for use in dealing with government which, by definition, has sanctions and powers to tax, legislate, adjudicate, and use other tools lacking in a voluntary polity such as the American Jewish community? The Jewish community to date has found it difficult to bridge the known to the accomplished with any consistency. The data reviewed here demonstrate a number of realities and a number of cautions in this regard.

The demographic trends are beyond dispute. The issue, then, is not what the facts are, but, rather, which trends, if any, are capable of being modified and what policies and strategies would be indicated as a result. I have argued here that no strategies can be introduced by a community which will affect or modify the size of the Jewish family. Exhortations, conferences, subsidies, threats, pleas - have all been tried, have failed, and will continue to fail.

There are, however, some trends which should lead to policy statements out of which strategies could be evolved. Kamerman and Woocher provide guidelines for appreciating the need for coalitions and creative linkages with government, where appropriate, while recognizing the limitations inherent in any implementation of policies in a voluntary community. It would seem deceptively easy to get consensus in the American Jewish community as to the policies needed which would have the greatest likelihood of being implemented through strategies and tactics, nationally and locally.

It is beyond the scope of this paper to detail the policy ramifications of all the trends identified earlier. Examples follow however, which define some parameters for the inevitable difficulties which await those who must engage in the process. The American Jewish community will be forced to confront harsh realities in the process of trying to plan and order priorities.

The inexorable growth of the elderly population with its predictable exponential need for adequate housing, health care, and social and recreational services will make greater and greater claims for attention and response. Simultaneously, there will be a growing need for low cost housing for the young; free or low cost Jewish education for new families and single parents; and increased subsidies for the agencies serving young couples, single parents, and new families, as possible strategies to counter plummeting affiliation rates, reduced numbers seeking Jewish education for their children, and increasing movement from the cities to the suburbs and beyond. Day care facilities and all the attendant services required to keep two-parent families relating to the Jewish community will be required on a large scale.

If the Jewish community cannot find the ways to create coalitions, unlock new resources, deal more effectively with government, and communicate better with individual Jews so as to evoke within them the idea of community as a desirable phenomenon, then the golden age which should await us will tarnish and prove instead to be a time of pain and dissolution.

Woocher's model of the seven principles which define "citizenship" in the Jewish polity provides a framework for the active voluntary entity we call the American Jewish community. The difficulty lies in the ordering of priorities in dispensing resources. This process cannot develop or take place outside of political realities in the larger society.

Foremost in this process must be the ability to accurately evaluate the "opinion-makers" in the Jewish community, and ascertain what their priorities are, and how they might be changed, if a need for change is indicated. (It should be noted that fund-raising trends in America suggest that a remarkably small and shrinking number of individuals account for the funds which are available for the Jewish "Treasury Departments" -- the allocation committees of the federations in America. In 1974, 8,600 gifts of $10,000 or more accounted for $343 million of the $669,800,000 raised that year, while in 1979 there were only 6,900 gifts of $10,000 and more which accounted for $221 million of the $481 million raised. Actually the Consumer Price Index in 1974 was 147.7 percent (1967=100) and had risen to 217.4 percent in 1979. In 1974 dollars, the total raised in 1979 was equivalent to $145,743,000. Too little weight has thus been given to the shrinking purchasing power of "Jewish dollars" when, according to Ceyfitz, Jews now control approximately 8 percent of the gross national product of some three trillion dollars. (122) I suggest that unless this group of "opinion-makers," which represent less than .003 percent of Jewish households in the U.S., agrees to defining the continuity and upbuilding of Jewish family life in America as the highest priority, there will be little radical change in the use of Jewish resources in the decade ahead.

Historically, the American Jewish leadership reflects Neusner's assessment, in that they often represent "a generation of public commitment to Jewish affairs and private neglect of Jewish life. Devotion to Jewish activities and indifference to their inner meaning and direction share the same national soul....People who lavish their best energies, their money, and their time upon Jewish activities also live lives remote from distinctive and particular Judaic meaning." (123) While Woocher has suggested that a change in attitude and practice is evident among young leadership, (124) their influence is not yet that great, and they tend to be more responsive to Israel and its needs than to the needs of Jews in America. What is the reality that awaits them?

Worldwide, all available evidence suggests that most Jews marry, stay married, have children, function reasonably well as parents, live long lives, work hard, behave responsibly, and have a sense of pride about being Jews. Most of them continue to want their children to be raised knowing they are Jews and, even though they are not sure how or why to do this, they want Jews to continue to exist as a group and, in most cases, even want their children to marry other Jews. Most Jews remain more comfortable socializing with other Jews and are sympathetic to, and concerned about, Israel.

Yet, for better or worse, most Jews in the world, when given the chance, will not move to Israel, even as they maintain an often near-mystical and non-rational relation to Israel. Many Jews who find little positive value in being Jews, nevertheless accept their existential reality as Jews. There is growing evidence of a readiness to join in corporate expressions relating to this acceptance by taking part publicly in demonstrations against anti-Semitism or in support of Israel. While no research has attempted to correlate the impact of these public actions upon Jewish family life, I would speculate that it enhances Jewish identity in the home and helps to cement inter-generational relationships while encouraging possibilities for the transmission of values.

Further, the development of peer support networks in America such as havurot, widows' groups, singles' and single parents' groups, step-parents' organizations, Jewish marriage encounters, family camping, "adopt a grandparent" programs, and the like, do have positive implications as transitional systems. They may, in some instances, come to substitute for extended and even nuclear families and provide new sources for value building and stabilizing Jewish families, albeit sometimes in new forms.

Some small beginnings in experimenting with these instruments for strengthening the Jewish family are evident in Israel and many countries throughout the world.

Ironically, the problems today are theoretically more capable of being controlled than were many of the causes of family disintegration in time past. The great historical destroyers and enemies of families - famine, war, infant and maternal mortality, epidemics, massive economic collapse - are largely memories today rather than realities (except for war in Israel). Thus <u>there is much to be optimistic about, precisely because the destiny of most Jews in the world is now in the hands of, and dependent upon the will, of Jews to live as Jews.</u>

IMPLICATIONS FOR POLICY AND ACTION

What then are the implications for policy and action? Paradoxically, perhaps, the Jews who serve Jewish families throughout the world can more easily agree on an agenda of common concern than set up means for concerted action. While approximately 45 percent of world Jewry live as Jews through totally voluntary affiliation and/or structures, the rest fall into a number of categories which, because of their status, require different policy responses. As I have stated, Jews in Israel represent over 20 percent of world Jewry and, through the existence of an autonomous government, can create policies which have both immediate and long range ramifications upon their psychological, ideological, cultural, and physical lives of the Jewish family. Outside of Israel, roughly 25 percent of Jews reside in countries where their status is at best marginal or, at worst, desperate. To speak of policy priorities for these Jews means first and foremost a policy or strategy of rescue. The remaining 10 percent of Jews most often have some official status as a community in their respective countries. The extent to which the organized Jewish community can respond to the needs of its Jews depends upon a combination of government and private funding, coupled with a mixture of Jewish community action with government support or sanction. These can have, of course, either a positive or negative effect. As an example, the Swedish Jew must first identify himself as a Jew to the government. The tax monies set aside for Jewish purposes are transferred to the Jewish community to fund the educational, cultural, social and religious services available to him under Jewish auspices. Those services are not, however, available to Jews who have not so identified themselves. Conversely, in French-speaking Canada, long established Jewish agencies have been absorbed into a government sponsored "nonsectarian" network. Further, Jewish schools continue to garner financial support by accepting "French Canadianization" as part of their Jewish educational agenda.

The status of professional Jewish communal workers will affect the seriousness with which strategies are effectuated. Although Jewish communal workers are not among the most highly respected professionals, their status is, nevertheless, much higher in

North America than elsewhere. The power, sanction, and authority of professionals is widely variable. This creates either problems or possibilities, depending on the strength of the professions in Jewish communal service. The position or role of the Jewish community itself is also an important variable. Finally, government policies vis-a-vis the family as an institution are shaped by the philosophies of the government, taking into account the status of the community and its professionals. Thus, the mechanisms for dealing with various trends, both positive and negative, will of necessity vary from country to country. In light of these considerations, strategies needed to strengthen Jewish families can be but faintly defined.

IX

AN AGENDA FOR THE AMERICAN JEWISH COMMUNITY

Despite these realities, I present the following suggestions taking into account the fact that the feasibility of their implementation can never be removed from the context of the society in which Jews reside.

1. The economic barriers to living fulfilled and creative Jewish lives must be lowered, so that no Jew is prevented from taking part in Jewish life and benefiting from its services because of the cost of those services. In some countries the high cost of Jewish education and affiliation has added to the downward trend in formal affiliation and calls have begun for innovative, sometimes revolutionary, ways of funding and providing these services. One funding technique might include selling bonds in the diaspora to raise funds for the diaspora. Such a project - selling bonds to support Jewish enterprises geared to enhancing Jewish life in America - is worthy of serious exploration.

2. Technological innovations must be widely utilized in the delivery of Jewish services. In America there are the beginnings of a Jewish television network, including a Jewish "Sesame Street"-type program; the increased publication of low cost books on "How to be Jewish;" subscription services for other educational resources and language study materials, including games, music tape cassettes, comic books, digests, and videotapes all dealing with Jewish concerns, "lifestyles," values, and specific teaching approaches. These resources must be expanded and made available wherever Jews live and in as many different languages as necessary.

3. Every means possible must be employed to encourage young Jewish people to marry Jews and to have children. This effort must begin at an early age through the development of special curriculum materials for educational institutions. Material geared to children, pre-adolescents, and adolescents must be developed in the forms of movies, discussion guides, magazine articles, video tapes, posters, programs for summer camps, and the like. (The example in England of developing a parallel to the American Coalition on Alternatives for Jewish Education is a healthy step in this direction.) The most sophisticated approaches must be identified, utilized, and carried out in order to help Jews heed the commandment "to be fruitful and multiply," even though strategies have not seemed to work in the past.

4. In some countries it will be necessary to establish alliances with other groups with shared concerns. Religious, ethnic, and racial groups with like-minded goals can be enlisted for joint actions on matters of common concern. In the United States, this may require a redefinition and reevaluation of understandings and expectations regarding church-state relations and the role and responsibility of government in granting tax credits, incentives, and support for sectarian purposes. In America, community agencies through and with the United Way have often been successful lobbyists for matters in this realm. While controversial, the same principle is involved vis-a-vis actions relating to tuition credits.

5. In the last decade, between 10 and 15 percent of world Jewry has migrated, mostly to America. Therefore, a policy and program of outreach embracing all Jews wherever they choose to live, must be seen as a matter of high priority. Ideological differences in organizations and conflicting conclusions arise from disparate premises regarding the future of Jewish life in the diaspora and in Israel. These conflicts will continue to influence policy decisions wherever they are made. If the result is to deny services to Jews and Jewish families because of where they have chosen to live, as with the argument regarding Soviet Jews and Israelis in America, one must remember that, ultimately, how Jewish families live as Jews remains as important today as it has been in the past. The quality of that life style must be enhanced without regard to where it is lived -- be it the diaspora or Israel.

For example, Israelis who have emigrated from Israel must not be treated as Jewish pariahs, left to fend for themselves, and regarded as outside the Jewish community. The future existence of their families as Jewish will have positive long range effects on all Jews, everywhere. The 'health' of their families is best assured through energetic efforts to respond to their needs. The history of Jewish life throughout the ages suggests the validity of this position.

6. It is a matter of high urgency to bring together a selected group of people to focus on policy issues for World Jewry. This group should include a representative sample of the 6900 largest contributors to Jewish "causes;" in America the young leadership of Jewish organizations and institutions, together with representatives from the rabbinate, international, national and local communal agency staffs, and academics. Using the 1980 White House Conference on Youth as a model, the goal should be first to convene a number of regional meetings with representative groups focusing on similar or the same policy issues.

The specific goal would be to move from regional meetings to a national meeting on "Jewish Family Policies" the conclusions of which would then be disseminated by every available means to Jews throughout the world. Thus strategies could be evolved worldwide which would respond to the central issue of Jewish family survival on a plane including, but broader than, the local organizational level.

*   *   *

Implicit in the premises of this book is the hope that insight will lead to action; and that the reader will become involved as a result. I have argued that some things are not as bleak as they appear, nor as new. Roles are changing, options for alternative lifestyles are more acceptable, life is more complex, the open society beckons.

A number of related trends have been identified which undermine the health of the family. Jewry today is engaged in a new kind of struggle of will, the struggle to want to continue to live as Jews, even as in most cases the disabilities imposed on us by societies in time past have been removed. For most Jews, it is not hard to be Jewish today because of what may befall us in the larger society. On the contrary, it is hard to be a Jew today precisely because it is so easy to be American, Canadian, English, French, or even Israeli, without reference to being Jewish. It is a kind of miracle that people outside of Israel meet together as Jews or that so many have chosen to remain Jewish. Admission to Western culture requires only that you be as you are -- not because you must, but because you want to. In short, one can do as much or as little as a Jew and still be accepted within the general society. Nevertheless, the Jews continue to face an anomalous situation.

As a people we have always lived in the tension produced by the coexisting ideologies of universalistic messianism and nationalism. Our past is replete with examples of individuals and communities seesawing on the "rocking board" of history. We have never achieved an ultimate balance. Neither have we given up the teeter-totter ride through time as a people -- even as individuals have fallen off, some to be bruised and to try again, others escaping to other games, in parks other than our own.

Some who have confronted the option of modernity, with all of its blandishments and potential benefits, have chosen to withdraw. There exists a small but dynamic group who have remained in the nineteenth century: the Hassidim. At the other end of the spectrum, are those who have removed themselves totally from the destiny of the Jewish people by disavowing any relatedness to past or present as Jews: these are the assimilationists. Most of us can be found somewhere in between these extremes. To a greater or lesser degree, and with varying need, opportunity, or desire, we try to actively join in the enterprise of the modern Jewish community, even as we seek to build individual lives within our families.

At least two points of view seem currently to be emerging which will contend for prominence and dominance. One could even speak of a coming battle between the "people of heat" and the "people of light." The people of heat will be motivated by their extreme interpretation of history and their evaluation of the present. Born of pessimism, anticipating a second Holocaust, viewing most gentiles as anti-Semites, seeing the future of the Jews in the bleakest and blackest of terms, they will fight for money and power to avert the anticipated doomsday of the Jews.

The danger signals and concerns which face us as a people must not be minimized or underestimated. They can, however, be seen in context, and I therefore choose the path of "the people of light." These Jews will be born of hope, and will be encouraged by options and opportunities for Jewish creativity. There exists today chances and choices for dynamic and ever more meaningful re-covenanting with those who remain Jews and choose to do so, not out of fear but out of desire. There are Jews who seek renewed forms of Jewish experience. The challenge is to create old-new ways to be Jewish and to set new priorities for all who serve the Jewish family.

It is clear that most Jewish families in the world will not return to traditional Jewish lifestyles, roles, and behaviors as a way of dealing with their difficulties. There are many, however, who are turning to the body of history and experience which may be called traditional, seeking linkage and connection to traditional though non-Orthodox ways. This extends beyond the small but visible number returning to Orthodox Judaism. Reform Jewry's selective return to some traditional practices is but one other example.

There are elements of Judaism which can be used as broad guidelines in developing both public policies and encouraging private commitments to enriched Jewish living. There are five informing principles at the heart of traditional Jewish life: 1) a sense of destiny; 2) a sense of discipline; 3) a sense of delineation of time and roles; 4) a sense of difference; 5) a sense of duty.

1) The covenantal imperative (following God's word because it is the Word) gives purpose and focus to traditional Jews. This belief system provides an anchorage of faith in an age of doubt

and a framework which gives sense and meaning to life. Having awareness of destiny provides a different perspective to the search for values and purpose and gives the security of relationship with the infinite to the finite human individual.

2) Out of this attachment comes the readiness and capacity to accept a life of discipline. The prescribed and proscribed gives structure to faith and, at its best, infuses the behavior which grows out of the acceptance of discipline of the law with joy and wonderment.

3) As a result of this union of a sense of destiny and the structures of discipline there has evolved in Judaism an approach to time which delineates the holy from the profane, the abiding from the mundane and, in so doing, enables people to approach the use of time and intergenerational relationships with predictability, familiarity, and responsibility.

4) In order for these values to survive, the need to be different becomes paramount. "Being different" must be sustained and permeate every aspect of one's lifestyle, home life, eating habits, the use of time, and the very nature of associations on a personal and community plane.

5) Thus there may arise an increased willingness to resume the responsibilities of being Jewish for oneself and towards Jews everywhere. My plea is for the non-traditional Jew to realize that the search for meaning in one's life cannot be the sole property of traditional Jews. Engaging in the search itself is a Jewish process, and this can best be done by building alliances within Jewish life and acting upon implemented strategies.

CONSCIOUS CHOOSING

The Jewish family must take conscious steps to live as Jews. Such conscious choice requires both time and opportunity for the family to set itself apart from others who have different goals, so as to be with other families with similar goals. Jews who wish to live as Jews must establish a rhythm of living in time with the rhythms of the Jewish calendar. They must not merely evoke the memory of the Jewish past through celebrating Jewish events, but must create their own Jewish family activities, and their own unique memories. The resulting emotional responses to such shared experience may be seen, tasted, heard, remembered, touched, and spoken of as being particularly Jewish moments. Taking a trip to Europe or through America and seeing Jewish places of historical interest, developing personal "familial" customs related to Jewish events create the memory bank drawn upon through life.

These experiences of linkage and bonding, which grow from shared joys or, as must happen in life, shared sorrows, may lead to the realization that living in a Jewish family is the natural way the Jew has of being human. Every family makes its own rituals. Father's nap in his favorite chair, shared verbal "codes" and private ways of communicating, the restaurant returned to again and again -- all are examples of the hundreds of ways, conscious and unconscious, that each family develops its own unique style. How much more significant when related to songs sung on Shabbat, the unique ways families have of making Kiddush, blessing bread, studying the portion of the week, discussing current events, etc.

The Jewish family can draw upon 120 generations which may nourish its present responses to life. The resulting amalgamation is always Jewish, yet changing as each generation contributes its own approaches to child-bearing, child-rearing, and inter-generational relationships. As has been noted above, the Jewish family's existence today is predicated on an act of will -- the will to be different from general society wherever Jews live. One cannot be Jewish in an active way without doing things that only other Jews do. However, there exists a broad spectrum of practice and ritual. Non-Orthodox Jews will not accept halachic proscription and prohibition as a basis for their Judaism. Thoughtful Jewish couples who wish to have Jewish grandchildren (which is a value-based desire to begin with) should know that, generally speaking, the more positively being Jewish is perceived by their children, the greater the likelihood of continuity. The Jewish family is NOT something for young children to vote in or out of existence. It is as much a necessity as is a wholesome diet. The child will have his or her opportunity later in life to renew the continuity with another act of will, or to opt out. Unfortunately, the evidence seems clear that fewer Jewish families in the future will opt for positive paths of remaining actively Jewish. Those that do will need all the reinforcement possible from institutions of the Jewish community.

JEWISH COMMUNITY INSTITUTIONS

Jewish organizations must understand the implications of the choices Jewish families must make if they wish to lead Jewish lives. Because being Jewish today is an act of will, families and institutions must define their primary concerns and priorities. Today, Jewish organizations do not agree on the idea of setting behavioral requirements or expectations as a precondition for offering services to their clients. The issue is indeed a delicate one.

Does an organization have a right to define a precommitment from a client or a member regarding the way they behave, that is to say, to act as Jews? Can a democratically-oriented system demand such promises as the price of service or admission? There are no easy answers to this question. Ideally, it should be possible to involve people in a process which results in a mutual consensus of expectations. Membership requirements are not a new concept. All societies set certain criteria as citizenship requirements. In reality, however, being Jewish in an open society is primarily a matter of self-definition for most Jews. Nevertheless, at the point that a family opts for membership in the Jewish community by asking for a service from it, that community, through one or another of its institutions, has the right to define expectations - albeit based upon the nature of the consensus arrived at by its constituents. Thus, a camp sponsored by a Jewish community center may be measurably different in its approach to Sabbath observance than one sponsored by a Conservative synagogue or Reform temple. The center camp, however, that ignores the Sabbath or accords it only perfunctory recognition, has not demanded the minimum responsibility from itself - which is to be involved in a serious Jewish enterprise and experience.

The same point applies to services offered by any Jewish organization or institution. Admission to Jewish communal life cannot be predicated on the dissolution of Jewish life. Let those for whom Jewish life is significantly "underwhelming," as a colleague so aptly stated, find their way to auspices which are not Jewish for whatever services they require. Most Jews in the diaspora live in open societies, which fulfill both group and individual rights. Jewish institutions have too often insufficiently understood the imbalanced equation in providing services to the individual at the expense of the group. A balance must be struck, since Jewish life can only be strengthened by those for whom and to whom it has significance. The process of the search for significance itself may thus be the lowest price of admission to receiving services from the Jewish community. Family services under Jewish auspices have the responsibility to ask Jewish questions of and outline Jewish consequences to their clients. Jews in an open society have the right to intermarry, but Jewish agencies in that open society have the obligation to take part in plans and programs which will reduce intermarriage rates. The case for zero population growth may today make sense for the world as a whole. However, to advocate its increased application among the first group of people to achieve zero population growth, a group which is also a post-Holocaust generation, is not an act which contributes to Jewish continuity.

The agenda can be lengthened. For each institution and family it may differ. Concern about the Jewish component gives legitimacy to an institution's demand for Jewish support. The solutions are not simplistic. For example, the existence of a hospital under Jewish auspices may be a sensible and highly urgent priority. However, its claim for Jewish funding priority should be justified in the context of the services it offers as related to Jewish life, as well as to its medical functions. For example, does the hospital have a Jewish chaplain, a chapel, a place for ritual circumcision, kashrut for those desiring it, etc.? These elements must be taken into consideration when deciding upon the disbursement of Jewish funds.

COORDINATION AND REORDERING PRIORITIES

There is every likelihood that many Jews will continue to be minimally involved in pursuing a vital and active Jewish lifestyle. Jewish community institutions will increasingly reflect this reality and, as a result, a split might well result in emphases. Every possibility exists that a large number of Jewish community institutions outside of Israel will have Jewish names and exist under Jewish auspices, yet minimize their Jewish purposes and services, and increasingly serve non-Jews. Jews attracted to such institutions will most likely come from among the most assimilated elements of the population.

To offset this trend, the institutions which remain or become strongly committed to Jewish purposes must seek each other out, regardless of their respective auspices. They must strengthen each other, share ideas, coordinate approaches, and conserve their abilities so as to make the most of their opportunities. Whether synagogue, community center, family service, or camp; whether rabbi, educator, or social worker -- neither their ideologies, sponsorship, nor professional differences should deter them from viewing each other as allies. Such institutions and those who serve them professionally will attract Jews who are ready to energize Jewish life. They will give to each other and gain from each other. Because they have hope in a future of being Jewish, they will have dreams and aspirations for institutional Jewish life. Because they will demand the best of themselves, they will expect the best from the institutions which serve them.

In Israel the struggle will take place on a different plane. Even there the desire of the secularist to find Jewish roots will intensify in the years ahead. Government concerns and services will respond in ways not possible outside of Israel. The issues will overlap increasingly, both in Israel and throughout the West. As a consequence, while there may be markedly fewer Jews outside of Israel in the decades ahead, they should be well served, even as they serve well in turn, by those institutions which are responsive and responsible to Jews and Jewish values.

The adventure of finding viable ways of human expression through Jewish paths will go on only as long as the vitality of Jews allows. Jews will continue to live as humans. A core will always live as Jews. None of us can predict the future; the most we can hope to do is to affect it. The evidence is mixed as to the health of Jewish life. However, its possibility remains open and includes many positive and viable options. While many Jewish individuals have not coped well in adapting to change, few would doubt the resiliency of the Jews as a people. Jews have adjusted with extraordinary flexibility to radical environmental and geopolitical realities in the 120 generations of their existence and continue to survive as Jews.

Yes, all life is metamorphosis; so, too, are individual lives and the life of the Jewish people. Some of us come from communities which will not respond in the decades ahead. For most, however, the strength and direction of our transformations will depend upon our roles in redeeming the best in ourselves and in our communities as Jews. We must listen to the sounds of history; some of which have been identified here. We, in turn, are responsible for the messages which will be written in the future.

FOOTNOTES

1. "Jewish Resourcefulness: A Response to Shrinking Resources" Hornstein Program in Jewish Communal Service. The Tenth Anniversary Milender Lecture in Jewish Communal Leadership. April 2, 1984, by Gerald B. Bubis.

2. Benjamin Schlesinger, The Jewish Family; a Survey and Annotated Bibliography. Toronto: University of Toronto Press, 1971.

3. "To Serve the Jewish Family" The Reconstructionist 1st. Vol. XLVI, January, 1981.

4. Trends and Issues in Jewish Social Welfare in the United States, 1899-1952. Edited by Robert Morris and Michael Freund. Philadelphia: Jewish Publication Society of America, 1966.

5. Schlesinger, The Jewish Family.

6. Gerald B. Bubis, ed. Serving the Jewish Family, New York: Ktav Publishing, 1977.

7. Graenum Berger, ed., Turbulent Decades: Jewish Communal Services in America 1957-58. New York Conference of Jewish Communal Service, 1980.

8. Frederick Morton, N.Y. Times Book Review. June 27, 1968.

9. Gerson Cohen, "Issues and Perspectives in Jewish Education." Jewish Education Association, 1980.

Jacob Rader Marcus, Jews in the Medieval World, a Source Book. 315-1791. Cincinnati: UAHC, 1938.

Ben Sasson and S. Ettinger, eds., Jewish Society Through the Ages. N.Y.: Schocken Books, 1969.

10. Gerson Cohen, Melton Center Newsletter. Fall, 1980.

Quoted in S.N. Herman, American Jewish Students in Israel, Jewish Social Studies, Vol. XXXIV, No. 1, January 1962.

11. R. L. Griswold, "History and Family Policy," Humanities Network, Vol. 4, No. 2 Summer 1980, State of California.

Samuel Joseph, Jewish Immigration to the U.S. 1881 - 1910, Columbia University, 1914.

12. Ibid. p. 2.

13. Ibid. quoted by Griswold p. 3.

Ibid. p. 7.

Robert Bachi, Population of Israel, Jerusalem Table 11:15 p. 184.

Ibid. Bachi Table 11:16 p. 184.

The problem of influencing atitudes and changing behaviors is a complicated one. I (with Lawrence E. Marks) discuss this in some depth in Changes in Jewish Identification: A Comparative Study of a Teen Age Israel Camping Trip, a Counselor-in-training Program, and a Teen Age Service Camp.

JWB NY 1975. See especially V. Kothandapani, "Validation of Feeling, Belief and Intention to Act," Journal of Personality and Social Psychology, Vol. 19, 1971, p. 321 for definitions and discussion of "conation," the term used for this process.

14. From Culture of Narcissism, C. Lasch, quoted by W. C. Capps, The Center Magazine Vol. XIII, No. 4 July/August 1980, p. 25.

15. Uri Bronfenbrenner in "Raising Children in a Changing Society," General Mills American Family Report, 1976-7, Yankelovitch et al., p. 9.

16. G. Cohen, Melton Center Newsletter p. 10.

D. Hartman Joy and Responsibility: Israel, Modernity and the Renewal of Judaism. Jerusalem: B.Z. Posner, pp. 75-80

17. Ibid. p. 70.

18. Ibid. p. 80.

19. Yankelovitch, p. 61.

20. S. Rosenberg, "Ethnicity With Religion and Religion Without Ethnicity," Conservative Judaism Vol. XXVII, No. 1, p. 72.

21. G.B. Bubis, "Confronting Some Issues in Jewish Continuity: The Response of the Profession, Journal of Jewish Communal Service Vol. LV. No. 1, pp. 10-22.

22. For a full discussion of cultural goal setting, see Magoroh Maruyama, AIP Journal, September 1973, pp. 346-356.

23. Ibid. p. 353.

24. R. Bachi "The Demographic Crisis of Diaspora Jewry," Background Paper for the President of Israel's Seminar, 1979 mimeo.

25. Ibid p. 8.

26. Ibid. p. 8.

27. Ibid. p. 9.

28. Ibid. p. 10.

29. Ibid. p. 11.

30. R. Block, "National Movements Among The Jews in Russia Toward the End of the 19th Century" Seventh World Congress of Jewish Studies Jerusalem, 1977 quoting R. A. Lewis, B. H. Roland, R.S. Clem, Nationality and Population Changes in Russia and the U.S.S.R., N.Y., London: Prager,, 1976.

A.J. Coale, B. Anderson, E. Harmon, "Human Fertility in Russia Since the 19th Century." Office of Population Research, Princeton University, 1979.

31. R. Bachi, "Demographic Crisis" p. 18.

32. E.A. Wrigley, "Reflections on the History of the Family Daedelus, 1973 p. 71. "The Process of Modernization and the Industrial Revolution in England" Journal of Inter-Disciplinary History Vol. 3, No. 1, 1972, pp. 225-229.

33. S. Della Pergola, "Demographic Perspectives of Mixed Marriages," p. 18 mimeo'd text, later published in Encylopedia Judaica Year Book, 1975/6 Keter, Jerusalem.

34. U.O. Schmelz, "Jewish Survival, the Demographic Issues," typescript p. 3, to appear in American Jewish Year Book, 1982.

35. Ibid. p. 4

36. A. Dubb, "Retrospect and Prospect in the Growth of the Jewish Community in the Republic of South Africa". Paper at the 5th World Congress on Jewish Studies, 1969.

37. F. Massarik, National Jewish Population Studies, CJF, 1971.

38. Dubb, op. cit. p. 15 typescript.

39. S. Della Pergola, Jewish Populations in Europe 1958-77 typescript p. 12.

40. Ibid. p. 13.

41. Ibid. pp. 14-17.

42. See especially Gideon Shimoni's Jews of South Africa, London, Oxford Press, 1981.

43. U.O. Schmelz - New Developments in the Natural Movements of the Jewish Populations in Israel Mimeo'd Jerusalem, 1978.

44. U.O. Schmelz - Jewish Survival, The Demographic Issues (Draft), Dec. 1978 Hebrew University of Jeruslaem, p. 65.

45. Sandra Rubenstein and Carol Mathews, Lesbian Jews - Reconciling to a Dual Identity HUC (unpublished) 1980.

46. Schmelz Jewish Survival p. 19.

47. Ibid. p. 20.

48. Ibid. p. 21.

49. S. Della Pergola - Demographic Perspectives table 9.

50. Israel Population by Age - Jerusalem Post Jan 26, 1981.

51. Della Pergola Demographic Perspectives, p. 6.

Della Pergola uses the term outmarriage and mixed marriage interchangeably to signify a marriage where one partner remains non-Jewish after marriage.

52. c.f. Among those who have re-acted to the rates have been Fred Massarik and Leonard. See F. Massarik "Intermarriage" - Moment Spring 1978.

Leonard Fein. "Save Consequences of Intermarriage" Jewish Social.

Dubb op. cit.

53. Goldscheider (discussion section).

Bachi, "Demographic Crisis," p. 52-56

54. c.f. G.B. Bubis, "To Serve the Jewish Family," Recon-structionist Vol. XLVI, January 1981, p. 15.

G.B. Bubis "The Jewish Community Center's Responsibility for the Needs of the Jewish Family," Journal of Jewish Communal Service Vol. LI, Spring 1975, p. 246.

55. M. Ozawa "Women and Work" Social Work Vol. 21, No. 6 Nov, 1976, pp. 455-462.

J.O. Beckett, "Working Wives: A Racial Comparison" Social Work Vol. 21. No. 6, Nov. 1976, pp. 463-72.

S.B. Kamerman Being Jewish and Being American Draft, Jan. 1981 mimeo'd - A.J. Committee

56. Jerusalem Post "Israel Population" Jan. 26, 1981.

57. Reported in an interview with the author March, 1981. Ms. Rasnik is the director of the Battered Women's Shelter in Herzliya, Israel.

58. Mimi Scarf - Battered Jewish Women: A Descriptive Study HUC unpublished, 1980.

59. Betsy Geller and Ellen Goldsmith, All in the Family: Intra-Familial Violence in the Los Angeles Jewish Community. HUC (unpublished) 1980.

60. Marcia Spiegel, The Heritage of Noah: Alcoholism in the Jewish Community Today. UHC (unpublished) 1979.

61. U.S. Census Data 1981, Bureau of Labor Statistics.

62. Della Pergola, Recent Demographic Trends, p. 21.

Roberto Bachi, Population of Israel, 1978, Jerusalem, p. 312.

63. Della Pergola, Recent Demographic Trends.

64. Bachi "The Demographic Crises" p. 26

65. Ibid. p. 26.

Ibid. p. 22.

66. Ibid. p. 22.

67. S. Goldstein "American Jewry: A Demographic Profile" American Jewish Yearbook, 1971.

68. S. Della Pergola "Patterns of American Jewish Fertility" Demography Vol. 17. 103, Aug. 1980.

The tables cited compare Jewish and non-Jewish rates through the immigration period, America's wars, the depression and show a consistent parallel pattern throughout.

69. Schmelz, U.O. and S. Della Pergola Demography of the Jews in Argentina and in Other Latin American Countries. 1974 Tel Aviv, Tel Aviv University. D. Horowitz Institute (in Hebrew).

70. Henripin, J. Trends and Factors of Fertility in Canada: 1961 Census Monograph Series.

71. B. Unterhalter & S. Della Pergola, First Data on Fertility. Jerusalem, Hebrew University Institute of Contemporary Jewry, South African Jewish Population Study, Advance Report 7. 1978.

72. S.J. Prais and M. Schmool. "The Fertility of Jewish Families in Britain". Jewish Journal of Sociology, Vol. 15. pp. 189-204.

73. Della Pergola and R. Bachi - op. cit.

74. C. Goldscheider - op. cit.

75. R. Bachi, "The Demographic Crisis" p. 51.

76. Lukasz Hirszowitz. The Soviet Census (1979): "New Data on the Jewish Minority" Research Report No. 5, Institute of Jewish Affairs in Association with the World Jewish Congress, London, April 1980.

77. S. Goldstein, "American Jewry."

78. R. Bachi The Decline of Fertility....

R. Bachi, "The Demographic Crisis," p. 48.

79. D. Friedlander and C. Goldscheider, College U. Press, 1979, 240 pp. The practice is still in process and linked to the 1981 130 percent rate of inflation as of this writing with approximately the same percentages holding, p. 120.

80. Report of Committee for Natality Problems, 1959, State of Israel p. 63.

Ibid. p. 126.

81. In a number of articles Ellenson has demonstrate that many Orthodox scholars of the last century were much more flexible than their contemporary counterparts in evolving humanly oriented responsa to questions of personal status in recognition of the pulls of modernity upon the Jew.

c.f. David Ellenson - "A Response of Modern Orthodoxy to Jewish Religious Pluralism: The Case of Esriel Hildesheimer Tradition Vol. 17, No. 4, Spring 1979.

D. Ellenson, and Robert Levine, "Rabbi Z.H. Kalischer and a Halachic Approach to Conversion," Journal of Reform Judaism. Summer 1981.

These are but two of many examples cited by Ellenson to demonstrate his thesis that flexibility is possible through utilizing the halachic process even though he finds no evidence today of the flexibility of rabbis 60 to 100 years ago.

82. Schindler is quoted in an interview "Reaching In Reaching Out." Moment Magazine, March 1978.
Ellenson indicates that support for Schindler's position has been forthcoming from scholars within the conservative movement. See "Accommodation, Resistance, and the Halachic Process: Jewish Civilization: Essays and Studies, Vol. 2, 1981. Reconstructionist Press.

"Boundary Maintenance, Identity Formation and the Role of Reform in selected German-Jewish Orthodox Response" HUC Annual - 1983.

Ellenson and Levine, "Rabbi Kalischer."

83. David Ben Gurion "Three Issues", Hapo-el Hazair" Vol. 27, 1941.

R. Bachi, "The Decline in Fertility: A National Danger" HaAretz, August 5, 1940.

84. Survey conducted in 1974 by D. Friedlander and C. Goldscheider unpublished - available at Institute of Contemporary Jewry, Hebrew University, Jerusalem.

85. Ibid. p. 187.

86. Ibid. p. 187.

87. D. Friedlander in B. Bereken ed. Population Policies in Developed Countries, N.Y. McGraw Hill 1974 quoting from the Report of the Committee for Natality Problems, 1966.

88. My recent study co-authored with H. Wasserman on Havurot in Los Angeles confirmed the very high consistency of observance among members of the major orthodox synagogue in Los Angeles, which as ascertained in interviews, was not the case in the same congregation 2 decades ago. See Havurot in 5 Synagogues in Los Angeles, G.B. Bubis, H. Wasserman, with Alan Lert. Jerusalem Center and HUC, 1982.

89. Friedlander and Goldscheider, "Population of Israel," p. 147.

90. While not germane to the body of this paper, it is incumbent that the Israel-Diaspora teams look at the ramifications vis-a-vis 1) Aliyah, 2) fundraising, 3) discourse between the two communities, with English less and less likely to be the lingua franca and 4) the resultant need for Diaspora Jews to master Hebrew, to identify but a few of the issues which will come to the fore as the inevitable Levantization of Israel becomes more apparent.

91. Friedlander and Goldscheider, "Population of Israel."

92. Ibid. p. 187.

93. Ibid. p. 187.

D. Friedlander in B. Bereken ed. Population Policies in Developed Counties N.Y. McGraw Hill, 1974, quoting from the Report of the Committee for Natality Problems, 1966.

94. c.f.Schmelz, see Jewish Survival Demographic Issues, Institute of Contemporary Jewry, Jerusalem, December 1978, typed script draft. Jewish Fertility and Contemporary America in Ritterband P. Editor, Dr. Sidney Goldstein, Schmelz, ibid. Della Pergola S. ibid. Patterns of American Jewish Fertility, Massarik National Jewish Population Study Data, ibid.

P. 123 ZPG For Women? quoted from Differential Fertility and Minority Group Survival, edited by M. Himmelfarb and V. Baras, Greenwood Press, 1977.

Schmelz and Della Pergola estimate that the Jewish population in the U.S. by 2000 will range between 4,974,000 and 5,571,000 depending upon a number of variables.

"U.S. Jewish Population Trends" U.O. Schmelz & Sergio Della Pergola, American Jewish Year Book, 1983, Vol 83. p. 179.

95. Uri D. Herscher, American Jewish Archives, Spring 1981

Goldscheider Demographic and American Jewish Survival, p. 130.

The population figures are drawn from P.R. Mended - Flohr and Jehuda Reinharz (ed.) The Jew in the Modern World, Oxford University Press, New York, Oxford. 1980.

Friedlander and Goldscheider, "Population of Israel," p. 147.

Friedlander and Goldscheider, p. 193. Schmelz, Della Pergola, Bachi, Friedlander and Goldscheider agree on the need of Jews to have more children. Their difference seems to be matters of degree rather than direction when projecting the ramifications for Jewish continuity. Some communities will undoubtedly disappear for all practical purposes in the next half century. This is not a new phenomenon in Jewish life and indeed when one consider that 30 percent of world Jewry resided in North and South America a scant 80 years ago, one can see why demographers attempt more longitudinal assessments together with their ramifications than is the propensity of social workers.

Table XVIII, World Jewish Population in Thousands, 1975, p. 542. The actual figure of Jews in Israel in 1975 was 2,959,000 which I have upgraded to 3,300,000 based upon figures available in 1982. The table was based on a work by Prof. Schmelz and showed a total population of 12,979,000 as of 1975 and excludes non-Jewish members of Jewish households.

96. Charles Morris, Varieties of Human Values, Chicago, University of Chicago Press, 1956, pp 9-12.

97. Allen Wheelis, The Quest for Identity, New York, W.W. Norton and Co., Inc. 1958, 177.

98. Muriel Pumphrey, Project of Values and Ethics: Working Definition of Terms, Curriculum Study, N.Y., Council on Social Work Education, 1957, p. 1. 104.

99. Muzafer, Sherif, The Psychology of Social Norms, N.Y. Harper & Bros., 1936, Chapter 1.

100. Robin M. Williams, Jr., Religion, Value Orientations and Inter-Group Conflict, from Readings in Social Psychology E.E. Maccoby, T.M. Newcomb, E.L. Hartley (eds). New York, Henry Holt & Company., p. 648.

101. Samuel C. Kohs, The Root of Social Work, New York, Assoc. Press, 1966, pp. 66-7.

102. Detailed discussion of this action - value patterning can be found in L. Rath, M. Harmin, S. Simon, Values and Teaching, N.Y., C.E. Merrill, 1966.

See the following as a frame of reference. Evelyn Duvall, Family Development, Family Social Welfare: Helping Troubled Families, N.Y. Atherton Press 1967. Otto Pollack, "A Family Diagnosis Model," Social Service Review XXXIV, March 1960.

David Friedman, Family Systems Therapy, Los Angeles, USC School of Social Work - Ph.D thesis, unpublished 1973.

103. Howard F. Stein and Robert HIll, "The Limits of Ethnicity" The American Scholar, pp. 118-198, Spring 1977.

104. M.N. Eagle "Jewish Life in the United States: Perspectives from Psychology" Jewish Life in the United States; Perspectives from the Social Sciences, J.B. Gittler, ed. N.Y., N.Y. University, Press, 1981.

105. H. Fingarette, The Self in Transformation, N.Y. Harper and Row, 1973.

106. Eagle, "Jewish Life in the U.S.," p. 109.

107. Bruno Bettelheim, The Informed Heart: Autonomy in a Mass Age, N.Y., Free Press, 1960.

Viktor Frankel, Man's Search for Meaning: An Introduction to Logotherapy, Boston, Beacon Press, 1962.

D. W. Winnicut "Transitional Objects and Transitional Phenomena in D.W. Winnicut, Through Pediatrics to Psychoanalysis, N.Y. Basis Books 1975, pp. 236

108. J.G. Robbin & E.L. Streuning. "Social Change Stress, and Illness: Selective Literature Review in T. Shapiro, ed. Psychoanalysis and Contemporary Science, Vol. 5, N.Y. International Universities Press, 1976, p. 57.

109. H.B.M. Murphy "Social Change and Mental Health" in Millbank Memorial Fund Conference, Causes of Mental Disorders - A Review of Epidemiological Knowledge, N.Y. Millbank Memorial Fund, 1961.

110. D. Sydiaha and I. Rootman, "Ethnic Groups Within Communities: A Comparative study of the Expression and Definition of Mental Illness" Psychiatric Quarterly, Vol. 43. 1969, pp. 131-146.

111. G. Klee, E. Spiro, A. Bahn & K. Gorwitz "An Ecological Analysis of Diagnosed Mental Illness in Baltimore" In R. Monroe, G. Klee and E. Brody, eds. Psychiatric Epidemiology and Mental Health Planning Psychiatric Research Report 22. American Psychiatric Association. 1967. pp. 107-148.

Stein and Hill, "Limits of Ethnicity," p. 187.

112. Bill Abrams, "Middle Generation Growing More Concern with Selves" Wall Street Journal, Thurs. Jan. 21, 1982, p. 25.

113. Yankelovich, Chart 2. p. 17.

114. The major writings on the Jewish community as a polity have been done by Professor Daniel Elazar, Dr. Jonathan Woocher and Professor Charles Liebman. See especially Daniel Elazar, Community and Polity: The Organizational Dynamics of American Jewry, Jewish Publication Society of America, 1976.

D. Elazar and Stepher R. Goldstein "The Legal Status of the American Jewish Community" in M. Fine and M. Himmelfarb (eds.). American Jewish Year Book, vol. 73, Phila. J.P.S. 1972.

Jonathan S. Woocher "The 'Civil Judaism' of Communal Leaders" in M. Himmelfarb, O.D. Singer (eds) Am. Jewish Year Book, Phila. J.P.S., 1981.

"Jewish Survivalism as Communal Ideology: An Empirical Assessment" Journal of Jewish Communal Service, Vol. 57 Summer, 1981, pp. 291-303.

"The American Jewish Polity in Transition" Forum 46/4, Winter, 1982, pp. 61-71.

Charles Liebman "Dimensions of Authority in the Contemporary Jewish Community", Jewish Journal of Sociology, Vol. 12, June 1970, pp. 29-37.

115. Woocher, "The American Jewish Polity in Transition", p. 63.

116. Ibid., p. 67.

117. See particularly the AJC Task Force on the 1980s paper by Sheila B. Kamerman, with comments by G. Bubis, B. Reisman, and C. Waxman, N.Y. 1981, 24 pp. and R.A. Zwerin and G.B. Bubis Strengthening the Jewish Family Through Community Support Systems, Council of Jewish Federations, N.Y. 1980 - 25 pp.

118. Kamerman, p. 15

119. Ibid. p. 16.

120. Ibid. p. 17.

121. Ibid. p. 18.

122. Giving Trends in U.S. among givers to the United Jewish Welfare Fund and United Jewish Appeal drives. Sources United Jewish Appeal, N.Y., 1982.

123. Jacob Neusner "Towards a Theory of University Studies in Judaism." Bernstein Conference on Jewish Studies, University of Rochester, N.Y., Feb. 22-24, 1976 proceedings. p. 14.

124. Woocher ibid. Jewish Survivalism

Sol Tax, "Jewish Life in the U.S." Perspective from Anthropology. J. Gettler ed., Jewish Life in the U.S. Perspectives from the Social Sciences, New York, NYU Press, 1981, p. 310.

CUMULATIVE BIBLIOGRAPHY

ABORTION

Right to life: absolute or relative? Editorial. Recon 47:5-6 F '82.

On abortion. B. Greenberg. il Had Mag 64:19-21+ O '82.

Jews and the abortion debate. J-A. Mort Jew Fron 49:7-9 Mr '82.

In brief. Editorial. Recon 47:5-6 D '81.

Abortion, halacha, and Reform Judaism. M. Washofsky. J Reform Jud 28:11-19 Fall '81.

What sex preselection can mean to Jews. H.J. Roberts. cond Jew Digest 27:3-6 O '81.

The halakhic status of the fetus with respect to abortion. R.S. Kirschner. Con Jud 34:3-16 Jl/Ag '81.

Resolution on abortion rights. Adapt. Ja 13 '81 Recon 47:47 Jl/Ag '81.

Abortion: religious differences and public policy. H. Siegman. Excerpt. Cong Mo 48:3-4 Je '81.

Legislation and abortion: the fight continues. pt 4: The constitution under attack. N.Z. Dershowitz. Cong Mo 48:8 Ap '81.

The right to do wrong: Reform Judaism and abortion. R.A. Block. J Reform Jud 28:3-15 S '81.

Abortion as holocaust: a colloquy. pt. a: A crippling analogy, E.G. Fisher; pt. 2: The victims of rhetoric, B. Brickner. Cong Mo 48:13-15 Ja '81.

The Jewish stake in abortion rights. A. Daum. Lilith No. 8:12-17 '81.

The deceitful equation: abortion as Holocaust. B. Brickner. Cong Mo 47:11-12 S/O '80.

Religion, Religious Beliefs, and Religious Practices Among Conservative Jewish Adolescents. Parker, Mitchell; Gaier, Eugene L. Adolescence, v. 15, n. 58, pp. 361-74. Sum 1980.

Adolescent Radicalism and Family Socialization. Niels Christiansen; Lea Vuori; Dennis Davis. Adolescence 1976, 11, 43, Fall 1976, 383-394.

ABORTION

An organic peer community - an experiment in Jewish teenage education. B. Lipnick. Address. Jew Ed 43:38-41+ W/Sp '75.

The new hermeneutic, language and the religious education of the adolescent. M.A. Ankoviak, sister. Rel Ed 69:40-52 JA/F '74.

ABUSE (other than alcohol)

Shelter for Jewish battered women. T.P. Halpern; C. Kaye. Adapt. Lilith No. 7:41 '80.

A Model of Therapy with Abusive and Neglectful Families. Susan Wells. Social Work, March 1981.

Child-rearing, religion, and abusive parents. K. Neufeld. Rel Ed 74:234-44 My-Je '79.

Innocent victims: NCJW Manual on Child Abuse and Neglect Programs. National Council of Jewish Women, New York, N.Y. Sep 1978. 84p.

Drug abuse. R. Samuel. Had Mag 54:18+ Mr '73.

Crime, punishment and narcotics. W.J. v. Heuvel. Address. Cong bi-W 40:6-9 Ja 26 '73.

Judaism and Drugs. Leo Landman, ed. Commission on Synagogue Relations, Federation of Jewish Philanthropies of New York, 1973.

ADOLESCENTS

Bribing delinquents to be good. Susan Seidner Adler. Commentary 72:55-61 O '81.

Abortion and Halakhah. R. Weiss. Letter. Reply S. Carmy. Trad 17:112-115 Sp '79.

Religious freedom and the American community. L. Pheffer. Adapt Jud 28:137-46 Sp '79.

Israel's abortion controversy. R.G. Weisbord. Cong Mo 46:11-13 Ap '79.

The facts of life. Reprint. Cong Mo 46:13 Ap '79.

ADOLESCENTS

The embryo and the soul. J. Cooper. Letter on R. Gordis's "Abortion." Reply R. Gordis. Mid 25:78-9 Ja '79.

Sixth session: The women's movement; Presentation L. Chanin. Discussion Z. Falk; H. Pilpel; A. Lichtenstein; L. Chanin; E. Rackman; L. Rabinowitz; A. Shapira; H. Squadron. Cong Mo 45:34-8 Mr/Ap '78.

Abortion. Major wrong or basic right. R. Gordis. Mid 24:44-9 Mr '78.

Dare man "play God?" S.J. Spiro. Jew Spec 43:13-16 Fall '78.

One family's story. Abortion controversy. D. Goldberg. Moment 3:52-4 D '77.

News and comments: Rise of DMC; Electoral reform; Abortion controversy; Marriage registrar; Soccer at the good fence; Keeping posted. Had Mag 58:33-6 Mr '77.

Performing abortions. M. Denes. Commentary 62:33-7 O '76.

Abortion and religious freedom. L. Pfeffer. Cong Mo 43:9-12 Je '76.

Abortion in Israel. Pros and cons. R. Furstenberg. Had Mag 57:20-1+ Mr '76.

Abortion: a challenge to Halakhah. B. Greenberg. Jud 25:201-8 Sp '76.

Psychiatric hazard in the HALACHIC disposition towards birth control and abortion: the role of the caseworker. M.H. Spero. J Jew Com Ser 53:155-64 W '76.

Abortion in traditional Jewish law. A. Steinberg. cond Jew Digest 22:9-12 N '76.

The religious freedom amendment. W. Pruden, Jr. cond Jew Digest 20:11-12 Je '75.

When does human life begin? D.M. Feldman. Keeping Posted 20:3-7 Ap '75.

Tay-Sachs and abortion legislation. R. Kushner. Nat Jew Mo 88:49-55 Jl/Ag '74.

Abortion and Jewish law. I. Schneider. Recon 40:26-30 Je '74.

ADOLESCENTS

Remembering us unto death. The rabbi confronts agonizing dilemmas.
W.B. Silverman. CCARJ 21:41-68 Sp '74.

How will our children answer? K.M. Mitzner. Ideas 4:12-16 No. 2
'74.

ADOPTION

Child welfare in Israel: an overview of institution care, foster home
care and adotpion. E.D. Jaffe. J Jew Com Ser 55:170-82 W '78.

When a Jewish family adopts a child. A.Kurzweil. cond Jew Digest
23:43-5 Ap '78.

What happens to the child hard to place for adoption. G. Winerman.
Address. J Jew Com Ser 53:192-200 W '76.

Adoption and after. I. Romm. Address. J Jew Com Ser 53:185-91
W '76.

A family of love. E. Oyserman. Had Mag 57:13 My '76.

Opening the sealed record in adoption - the human need for
continuity. R. Pannor; A.D. Sorosky; A. Baran. Address. J Jew Com
Ser 51:188-96 W '74.

Stranger than fiction. J. Pascal. cond Jew Digest 19: 61-2 O '73.

The children of Black-Jewish alliances. J. Schatz. cond Jew Digest
18:67-70 My '73.

From oriental orphans to Orthodox Jews. B. Friedman. cond Jew
Digest 18:63-4 Mr '73.

AGED AND AGING

Jewish ethnicity and aging. M. Stambler. J Jew Com Ser 58:336-42
Sum '82.

The life you gave me. B. Howland. Commentary 74:43-58 Ag '82.

Helping elderly victims of crime. E. Reingold. Address. J Jew Com
Ser 58:245-8 Sp '82.

A family education program for Soviet Jewish seniors. P. Frankel; M.
Golant. Address. J Jew Com Ser 58:223-30 Sp '82.

AGED AND AGING

Aging quiz. Keeping Posted 27:15 Ap '82. kp Interview: Starving in America. L. Schwartz-Nobel. Keeping Posted 27:13-14 Ap '82.

Special issue Keeping Posted 27: Ap '82.

Frontiers of service to the aging. B. Warach. J Jew Com Ser 59:26-34 fall '82.

The parents went to camp and the children stayed home. C. Neff. il Jew Mo 96:46-7 D '81.

University Centennial Edition: Family Treatment in Social Work. Elizabeth McBroom, Ed.; and others. Social Work Papers of the School of Social Work, University of Southern California, v. 16, Spr 1981.

The aged. S.K. Wohlgelernter. Letter. Reply S. Siegel. Jew Spec 46:59+ Sp 81.

Toward an age-blind society. B.I. Forman. Recon 46:20-5 Ja '81.

Social Work with the Aged: Principles of Practice. Abraham Monk. Social Work, January 1981.

Day care: its value for the older adult and his family. F. Wish. Address. J Jew Com Ser 47:174-80 W '80-1.

The aged and human values. S. Seymour. Jew Spec 45:19-22 W '80.

The Aged and their Adult Children. Samuel Lerner. CJF-General Assembly, 1980.

Project VISA - meeting the needs of the visually impaired senior adult. M. Belkin. Address. J Jew Com Ser 57:26-9 Fall '80.

Cooperative planning for discharge from geriatric institutional care. M. Schneider. Address. J Jew Com Ser 56:358-60 Sum '80.

Reaching out to the aging through vocational services. C. Fogel. Address. J Jew Com Ser 56:341-3 Sum '80.

The most wished-for chronic ailment. T. Weiss-Rosmarin. Editorial. Jew Spec 44:8 W '79.

Too old for aliya? Israel Digest 22:16 F 24 '79.

AGED AND AGING

Tokenism in senior citizenship. B.I. Forman. Cong Mo 46:18 Je '79.

Growing old. M. B. Greenbaum. Letter. Moment 4:4+ Mr '79.

Attack on ageism: the Jewish stake in the work ethic. B.I. Forman. Recon 44:17-24 Ja '79.

The move of Jacob Portman. T. Cottle. Moment 4:51-4 N '78.

The smell of time. Portraits of the aging. Millie Portman; Bernice Wein; Rose Orlovsky; Ella Crown. T. Cottle. Moment 3:29-38 Mr '78.

The role of the community center in meeting the health needs of the aged: an overview. B. Rubin. Address. J Jew Com Ser 54:32-8 Fall '77.

Housing for the elderly. S. Spiegler. J Jew Com Ser 54:85 Fall '77.

Will you fit into your synagogue? D. Gorin. Un Syn Rev 30:16 Sum '77.

Judaism and gerontology. B. Blech. Trad 16:62-78 Sum '77.

The Gerda Charles view: Where does real charity begin? Jew Ob 26:18 S 22 '77.

The aging of American Jewry. G.E. Johnson. cond Jew Digest 23:76-8 S '77.

Helping Older Adults Help Themselves. William S. Bernstein. Jewish Community Center Program Aids, Vol. XXXVIII, No. 1, Winter 1976/77, pp. 13-15 & 24.

Serving the Aged and Neglected. David Wolper; Mae Cowen. Sh'ma, Vol. 7, No. 121, November 12, 1976, pp. 3-4.

Search for Jewish self-fulfillment. C. Forse. Un Syn Rev 28:5-7 W '76.

Leisure time preference and participation of senior adults with some college education. E. Simon. J Jew Com Ser 52:211-12 W '76.

The poor Jews. R.L. Kern. Jew Spec 41:50 W '76.

A kosher busing program. S. Spiegler. J Jew Com Ser 53:208 W '76.

AGED AND AGING

Small group home projects for the elderly. M. Schneider. J Jew Com Ser 53:88-92 Fall '76.

The Jewish Aging: Problem Dimensions, Jewish Perspectives, and Unique Role of the Family Agency. David Zeff. J Jew Com Ser 53:81-87 F '76.

A day-hospital program for brain-damaged confused geriatric patients. L.J. Noveck. Address. J Jew Com Ser 53:74-80 Fall '76.

The Jewish aging: problem dimensions, Jewish perspectives, and the unique role of the family agency. D. Zeff. J Jew Com Ser 53:81-7 F '76.

The mentally aged: reordering priorities. J.S. Edelson. Address. J Jew Com Ser 53:63-73 F '76.

A personal look at project Ezra. T. Brandriss. Response 10:135-41 Sum/Fall '76.

Aharei kiddushin: a proposal for mid-life recognition ceremonies. A.M. Lewis. CCARJ 23:41-6 Sp '76.

The aging of the Jewish community. G.E. Johnson. cond Jew Digest 21:38-40 My '76.

Being old isn't living. M.B. Levy. Nat Jew Mo 90:20+ Mr '76.

You and your aging parent: a laboratory approach. S. and E. Bayer. J Jew Com Ser 52:174-81 W '75.

Nursing home reforms: A J Congress' role. N. Levine. Cong bi-W 42:3-4 F 21 '75.

My saintly step-mother. A. Blinderman. Jew Digest 20:66-8 F '75.

Synagogue program for the aging. Adapt that thy days may be long in the good land: a guide to programs for synagogues. 2 pts. cond Jew Digest 20:37-43 Jl; 51-6 Ag '75.

The role of the rabbi in an Orthodox long-term geriatric hospital. L.J. Novick. Address. J Jew Com Ser 51:373-80 Sum '75.

Golden age. B. Howland. Commentary 59:51-9 Ap '75.

AGED AND AGING

The case of Geza Kun, 1058 Simpson Street. R. Kestenbaum. Nat Jew Mo 89:38+ Mr '75.

Care for the aged; a positive Jewish approach. J.S. Cohen. Jew Life 41:17-20 Autumn '75.

Growing up -- some new influences. B.M. Foss. Address. Pat Prej 9:8-11 Ja/F '75.

Some Differences between Elderly People Who Use Community Resources and those Who Do Not. Norman Rosenzweig. Journal of the American Geriatrics Society, 1975, 23, 5, May, 224-233.

The changing focus in geriatric care; role of the social worker in rehabilitation, restoration, return to community. S. Feinberg. Address. J Jew Com Ser 51:197-201 W '74.

Comment on changing focus in geriatric care-discharge, pro and con. S.C. Olstein. Address. J Jew Com Ser 51:202-5 W '74

Compulsory retirement: a vehicle for discrimination. E.S. Fox. Cong bi-W 41:6-8 D 27 '74.

Consideration in planning services for the elderly. J. Solomon. J Jew Com Ser 51:90-4 Fall '74.

Rehousing elderly Jews. M. Hochbaum. Cong bi-W 41:11-13 F 8 '74.

Old-age education: an approach to dealing with aging and retirement. I.K. Ogawa. Rel Ed 69:593-611 S/O '74.

Community action and transportation for the elderly. L.E. Blonsky. J Jew Com Ser 51:313-21 Sum '74.

Feeding the soul; luxury or necessity? R. Greenwald. Jew Life 41:25-8 Sum '74.

Help for the blind and the aged. Jew Ob 23:19 My 17 '74.

A Jewish home for the aged provides a learning experience for nursing students. G. Safier; E.S. Oles. J Jew Com Ser 50:257-64 Sp '74.

Environment and the Well-Being of Elderly Inner-City Residents. M. Powell Lawton; Jacob Cohen. Environment and Behavior 1974, 6, 2, Jun, 194-211.

AGED AND AGING

Cash for the aged poor. S.D. Stillman. Jew Digest 18:17-20 F '73.

Portrait in poverty. D. Rabinowitz. Extract her The other Jews: portraits in poverty. Jew Digest 19:59-64 N '73.

The use of social group work with older adults: Promises and problems, principles and practices. N.N. Garoff. Address. J Jew Com Ser 49:318-23 Sum '73.

Social work implications in intergenerational problems with aging parents. B.G. Simos. J Jew Com Ser 49:238-45 Sp '73.

Adult Children and Their Aging Parents. Bertha G. Simos. Social Work 18, 3, 78-85, May 1973.

Poor aged get legal aid. S. Spiegler. J Jew Com Ser 49:254 Sp '73

Elderly to elderly. R. Seligman. Had Mag 55:16-18 S '73.

The Jewish poor: new facts. N. Levine. Cong bi-W 40:3-4 F 9 '73.

How can we respond to the needs of the elderly? B. Warach. Jew Life 40:17-24 Ja '73.

The other Jews: the poor among us. A.G. Wolfe. Keeping Posted 17:3-6 Ja '73.

Hearing our elderly. E.L. Brooks. Address. J Jew Com Ser 50:189-94 W '73.

Enhancing independent living for the Jewish aged; the role of the Jewish communal worker. C. Miller. J Jew Com Ser 50:174-9 W '73.

Are we underestimating the resources of the elderly? L.E. Blonsky. J Jew Com Ser 50:180-3 W '73.

A city-seder program for senior citizens. H. Rappaport. Address. J Jew Com Ser 50:184-8 W '73.

ALCOHOLISM

Fighting alcoholism. M Calarino. Letter. Present Tense 9:3-4 Sp '82.

ALCOHOLISM

Hard drinking. M. Spiegel. Present Tense 9:14-17 W '82.

Jews and alcohol. W. Duckat. Jew Spec 46:19-22 W '81.

Developing awareness of chemical use in the Jewish community. B. Friedman. Address. J Jew Com Ser 47:185-8 W '80-1.

Sexism and Treatment of the Female Alcoholic: A Review. Marguerite L. Babcock and Bernadette Connor. Social Work, May 1981.

Jews and alcoholism. M.C. Spiegel. cond Jew Digest 26:6-12 F '81.

Jewish alcoholics. Letter. Nat Jew Mo 95:54 F '80.

Jews and booze. M.C. Spiegel. Had Mag 62:16-17+ N '80.

The Jewish alcoholic. From kiddush to cocktails. G. Youcha. Nat Jew Mo 94:16-18+ D '79.

An Experiment in the Treatment of Alcoholics in Israel. Menachem Amir; Pnina Eldar. Drug Forum: Journal of Human Issues, vol. 7, no. 2, pp. 105-19, 197, 1978.

The drinking Jewish woman. E.L. Hornik. Extract her The drinking woman. Jew Digest 24:36-40 N '78.

Why don't Jews drink? S. Spiegler. J Jew Com Ser 54:84 Fall '77.

Synthesis. R. Stratton; A. Paredes. J Psychology and Jud 1:77-8 Fall '76.

The giant killer: drink and the American way. A. Kazin. Commentary 61:44-50 Mr '76.

Soldiers who take a nip. Jew Ob 23:17 F 22 '74.

BIRTH - see Fertility

BIOETHICS - see Ethics

CHILDREN

Toward Reducing Recidivism in Foster Care. Norman H. Block. Child Welfare, vol. 60, no. 9, pp. 597-610, nov 1981.

CHILDREN

Family Day Care in the United States: Family Day Care Systems. Final Report of the National Day Care Home Study. Volume 5. Janet Grasso; Steven Fosburg. Abt Associates, Inc., Cambridge, Mass.; Center for Systems and Program Development, Inc., Washington, D.C.; SRI International, Menlo Park, Calif. 1 Aug 1980, 185p.

Creating Americans at the Educational Alliance. Cary Goodman. Journal of Ethnic Studies. 1979, 6, 4, Winter, 1-28.

Ministry to parents of little children. L.W. Barber; J.T. Hiltz. Rel Ed 74:263-9 My-Je '79.

The right of the Jewish child to be Jewish. M. Ginsburg. Rel Ed 74:287-94 My-Je '79.

U.N. declaration of THE RIGHTS OF THE CHILD. Recon 45:6 Mr '79.

The latency child -- more than meets the eye. M. Levine; C.W. Wolf. Address J Jew Com Ser 55:255-9 Sp '79.

Special education and remediation: resources and assistance. M.M. Schnaidman. Ped Rep 27:20 W '76.

Letter (Where are our children?) J. Aronson. Moment 1:74 My/Je '76.

Fear and fantasy; new psychological approach to the child facing major surgery. A. Stone il. Had Mag 57:14-15+ Mr '76.

An approach to the treatment of children in group residences. J.L. Taylor. Address. J Jew Com Ser 52:286-92 Sp '76.

Home-SAFE: A New Approach in Day Care for the Young Child. Maurine Kornfeld. Apr 1974, 13p.; Paper presented at the Annual Meeting of the American Orthopsychiatric Association (51st, San Francisco, California, April 1974).

What's Jewish about Jewish child care? H. Goldstein. J Jew Com Ser 49:309-12 Sum '73.

On the birth of a daughter. D.I. Leifer. Response 18:91-100 Sum '73.

CHILDREN

The Jewish mother vs. the kibbutz. Extract Jew Digest 18:63-4 Ag '73.

Making room for children. G. Brown, Jr. Rel Ed 68:401-6 My/Je '73.

The Children You Gave Us: A History of 150 Years of Service to Children. Jacqueline Bernard. Jewish Child Care Association of New York, N.Y. 1972, 186p.

COLLEGE STUDENTS

From Berkeley to Jerusalem. H. Goldberg. Mid 28:1-3 Je-Jl '82.

Coping 101: a mini course in what to take to college. C. Kur. Moment 6:55-7 O '81.

College freshman, Jewish and non-Jewish, compared. J Jew Com Ser 58:78 Fall '81.

For the sake of tikun olam. G. Serotta. Jew Spec 46:11-12 Sum '81.

Report from Boston. The unaffiliated. S. Rothchild. Present Tense 7:15-17 Sum '80.

A Profile of the Jewish Freshman: 1980. David E. Drew; and others. Higher Education Research Inst., Inc., Los Angeles, Calif. 1981, 191p.

Jewish students: changing attitudes. J. Groner. Cong bi-W 41:12-13 N 22 '74.

It doesn't have to be college. M. Effron. Nat Jew Mo 89:60-2 N '74.

New present or troubled future? L. Kahn. Recon 40:7-9 O '74.

Jewish ignorance vs. Jewish identity on campus. S. Spiegler. J Jew Com Ser 51:96-7 Fall '74.

The end of the movement. D. Twersky. Letter. Jew Spec 39:69-70 Sum '74.

Jewish psychosocial identity of youth; a programmatic approach. B.J. Goldberg; A. Weinstein. J Jew Com Ser 50:66-74 Fall '73.

COLLEGE STUDENTS

Where the boys are. A.J. Wolf. Nat Jew Mo 88:28+ S '73.

COMMUNITY CENTERS, JEWISH

Toward a definition of tomorrow's community center. P. Abrams. Address. J Jew Com Ser 59:161-9 W '82.

The senior center and the dying. F. Kaplan. Address. J Jew Com Ser 58:123-32 W '81-2.

The roll of Jewish community center camping programs in the modification of Jewish identity. G.B. Bubis; L.E. Marks. Adapt their Changes in Jewish identification. J Jew Com Ser 52:68-72 Fall '75.

Institutionalization of political action among senior adults in a community center. S. Kornblum; C.A. Lieberman. J Jew Com Ser 51:251-9 sp '75.

The Jewish community center's responsibility for the needs of the Jewish family. G.B. Bubis. Address. J Jew Com Ser 51:246-50 Sp '75.

Frustrations of a non-professional, recalled in a state of approximating tranquility. I. Resnikoff. J Jew Com Ser 50:275-7 Sp '74.

The revolt against social work in the Jewish community center. J Jew Com Ser 50:223-7 Sp '74.

COMMUNITY LIFE, JEWISH

Community organization in Jewish communal work. M.B. Mogulof. J Jew Com Ser 59:126-31 W '82.

The Chevra - an influential factor in Jewish community life. H. Katchen. Con Jud 35:67-73 W '82.

Jewish education under communal auspices. B. Rand. Jew Ed 50:18-23 Sum '82.

The planning process in the Jewish family agency; "tailoring" services to community needs. E. Del Monte. Address. J Jew Com Ser 59:83-7 Fall '82.

Is the Jewish community (truly) treating the Jewish family? E. Nulman. Address. Adapt J Jew Com Ser 59:66-72 Fall '82.

COMMUNITY LIFE, JEWISH

An Orthodox leader speaks out for mutual responsibility. Editorial.
Recon 46:4-5 Ja '81.

The Sociology of American Jewry: The Last Ten Years. Samuel C.
Heilman. Annual Review of Sociology 1982, 8, 135-160.

The professor and the Jewish community. A. Dashefsky. Letter. Jew
Spec 46:59+ W '81.

The "Jewishness" of young Jewish communal leaders. S. Spiegler. J
Jew Com Ser 58:80-1 Fall '81.

Toward a theory of modern Jewish social control. N.B. Mirsky. Jud
30:444-50 Jall '81.

The Jewish community. Editorial. Recon 47:6+ Jl/Ag '81.

Open forum: The graying of the American Jewish community:
implications of changing family patterns for communal institutions.
R.G. Monson. Con Jud 34:52-6 Jl/Ag '81.

Jewish Survivalism as Communal Ideology. Jonathan S. Woocher. J
Jew Com Ser S 1981.

Professional trends in Jewish communal practice in America. G.B.
Bubis. Address. J Jew Com Ser 57:304-11 Sum '81.

To serve the Jewish family. G.B. Bubis. Address. Recon 46:13-19 Ja
'81.

The family is very much alive. H. Davis. Israel Scene 22-3 D '80.

The challenge of outreach; turning on turned off Jews. R.J. Israel.
Address. J Jew Com Ser 56:306-9 Sum '80.

The Jewish community of the 1980s. L.J. Fein. Address. J Jew
Com Ser 57:9-16 Fall '80.

The impact of feminism on American Jewish communal institutions.
J Jew Com Ser 57:73-9 Fall '80.

Jewish Life: a statement of purposes. Y. Jacobs. Jew Life 3:45 Sp
'80.

The Jewish component in Jewish communal service - from theory to
practice. G.B. Bubis. Address. J Jew Com Ser 56:227-37 Sp '80.

COMMUNITY LIFE, JEWISH

Jews and Judaism in the 20th century. S.D. Temkin. Jew Spec 44:23-30 Fall '79.

The Jewish family and Jewish communal service: a crisis of values. B. Reisman. Address. J Jew Com Ser 56:35-9 Fall '79.

Wanted dead or alive. J. Neusner. Moment 4:61-4 Ja F '79.

Ethnicity in Phonological Variation and Change. Martha Laferriere. Language, vol. 55, no. 3, pp. 603-17. Sep 1979.

From my vantage point. A.J. Levine. Address. Un Syn Rev 30:8+ W '78.

The Jewish community as a force for Jewish continuity: an historical perspective. J. Prawer. J Jew Com Ser 55:23-43 Autumn '78.

Confronting some issues in Jewish continuity: the response of the profession. G. Bubis. Address. J Jew Com Ser 55:10-22 Autumn '78.

Mishpokhe: A Study of New York City Jewish Family Clubs. W.E. Mitchell. The Hague: Monton, 1978.

The unique Jewish family agency. M. Bernstein; F. Perlmutter. J Jew Com Ser 54:314-20 Sum '78.

Women in the Jewish communal structure. A.G. Wolfe. ADL Bull 35:5 S '78.

An Interpretation of the Jewish Counterculture. David Glanz. Jewish Social Studies, 1977, 39, 1-2, winter-spring, 117-128.

American Jewish Families: The Occupational Basis of Adaptability in Portland, Oregon. William Toll. Jewish Journal of Sociology, 1977, 19, 1, June, 33-47.

The Community Variable in Jewish Identification. Bernard Lazerwitz. Journal for the Scientific Study of Religion, 1977, 16, 4, Dec, 361-369.

A Multi-media Presentation of the History of the Jews of Michigan: Part I, 1640-1880, Part II: 1880-1940. Final Report. Wayne State Univ., Detroit, Mich., 1977, 103p.

COMMUNITY LIFE, JEWISH

The Impact of Family Formation Patterns on Jewish Community Involvement.   George E.   Johnson.   Analysis, No.   60,   November-December 1976, pp. 1-5.

The changing Orthodox Jewish Community.   G.G. Krauzler.   Tradition, Vol. 16, #2, Fall 1976, pp. 61-73.

Social work and the Jewish community center.   C.S. Levy.   Address. J Jew Com Ser 53:44-51 Fall '76.

The changing Jewish community.   B. Olshansky.   Address. J Jew Com Ser 53:29-43 Fall '76.

Needed -- a new institution.   M. Levin.   J Jew Com Ser 53:52-62 Fall '76.

The case for conflict in communal life.   S.M, Cohen.   Response 10:5-12 Sum/Fall '76.

America -- a novum in Jewish experience.   R. Gordis.   Jud 25:261-9 Sum '76.

The Jewish family agency and the problem of poverty among Jews. Address.   S. Lerner.   J Jew Com Ser 52:293-300 Sp '76.

Poverty in America.   Letter.   G.G. Eisenberg.   Reply S. Lebergott. Commentary 61:26-8 Ja '76.

Recruitment and training of personnel for central Jewish education agencies.   N.H. Winter.   Jew Ed 43:26-32 W/Sp '75.

Think tank -- Jewish style.   P. Dickson.   Present Tense 2:15-17 W '75.

On getting it together -- in a fairly together place. M. Goldstein.   J Jew Com Ser 52:163-73 W '75.

Comment.   Saul Hofstein.   J Jew Com Ser 52:1 F '75.

The social work function of the Jewish community center.   J.M. Carp.   Address.   J Jew Com Ser 52:43-58 fall '75.

Jewish communal services feel recession.   S. Spiegler.   J Jew Com Ser 52:107 Fall '75.

COMMUNITY LIFE, JEWISH

The Jewish family service agency: its functions in the Jewish community. P.M. Glick. J Jew Com Ser 51:389-94 Sum '75.

Jewish Values in the clinical casework process. Pauline D. Goldberg. J Jew Com Ser 51:3 '75.

Teaching undergraduates about Jewish communal agencies; the case for experience-based learning. S. Klarreich. J Jew Com Ser 51:280-4 Sp '75.

Rejoinder to the responses to The Report of the Commission on Structure, Function and Priorities of the Organized Jewish Community. A.J. Kutzik. J Jew Com Ser 51:295-9 Sp '75.

Changing lifestyles, the Jewish family and the Jewish community. M.S. Shapiro. Address. Cong Mo 42:14-21 S '75.

Jewish communal workers: a new spirit. Editorial. Recon 40:5-6 Ja '75.

An Analysis of Cultural Patterns among Orthodox Jews as Contrasted to those of Select White Middle Class Christian Americans. Florence Brenner; and others. Rutgers, The State Univ., New Brunswick, N.J. Inst. for Intercultural Relations and Ethnic Studies. 1975, 71p.

Commitment and freedom: a paradox in service to the Jewish family. F. Berl. Address. J Jew Com Ser 51:151-61 W '74.

The yearly cycle of the Ioannina Jews. R. Dalven. Con Jud 28:47-53 W '74.

Death and Jewish tradition. J.C. Robertson. cond Jew Digest 20:57-61 N '74.

Comment on "The crisis in Jewish life." T. Kanner. J Jew Com Ser 51:28-31 Fall '74.

To whom it may concern? Editorial. Recon 40:3-4 Mr '74.

What "community" is all about. Editorial. Recon 40:4-5 Je '74.

Twentieth century Judaism in America in relation to the social and religious environment. A.A. Lor. Rel Ed 69:316-33 My/J '74.

COMMUNITY LIFE, JEWISH

The Study of Poverty in the Jewish Community, City of New York. Joel Rosenshein; Sol Ribner. Hassidic Corp. for Urban Concerns, Brooklyn, N.Y. 1973, 110p.

Toward Enriching the Quality of Jewish Life; The Role of the Jewish Family and Child Agency. T. Isenstadt. J Jew Com Ser pp. 31-39, Fall 1973.

The Role of the Synagogue. Gerald B. Bubis. CCARJ Autumn 1973.

Jews in the Changing Urban Environment. E. Ginsberg. Con Jud 27:4 Summer 1973, pp. 12-23.

CONVERSION

Ben/Bat Avraham avinu: reflections on the convert to Judaism. H.L. Horowitz. Con Jud 36:71-3 Fall '82.

More than "information" in the Jewish information class. M.D. Shapiro. J Reform Jud 29:56-64 Sum '82.

The status of a non-Jewish spouse and children of a mixed marriage in the synagogue. K. Abelson. Con Jud 35:39-49 Sum '82.

Religious conversion and the revolt model for the formation of Israel. J. Milgrom. J Bib Lit 101:169-76 Je '82.

Reader's Letters; The conversion controversy. Israel Scene 33-4 Ap '82.

Ger-toshav: reviving an ancient status. R.M. Brauner. Recon 48:28-30 Ap '82.

Conversion as a foundation of religious education. M.C. Boys. Rel Ed 77:211-24 Mr-Ap '82.

Welcome Jews by choice. S.C. Lerner. Letters. Moment 7:8-9 Ja-F '82.

Who is a convert? B. Sofer. Israel Scene 13-16 Ja '82.

Some involuntary conversion techniques. L.L. Schwartz; N. Isser. Jew SS 43:1-10 W '81.

Jews for Jesus -- Mandelstam, Pasternak, Weil, M. Syrkin. Mid 27:14-18 N'81.

CONVERSION

Conversion nurture and educators. T.H. Groome. Rel Ed 76:482-96 S-O '81.

Becoming a Reform Jew: problems and prospects. S. Huberman. J Reform Jud 28:58-67 Sum '81.

Preparation for marriage to a Jew. L. Simon. J Reform Jud 28:68-75 Sum '81.

Rabbi Z.H. Kalishcher and a halachic approach to conversion. R. Levine; E. Ellenson. J Reform Jud 28:50-7 Sum '81.

Public conversion. D.C. Sasso. Letter. Moment 6:6-7 Jl-Ag '81.

The paradox of Reform conversion. D. Cohn-Sherbok. J Reform Jud 27:83-5 W '80.

What happens after conversion? L. Byard. cond Jew Digest 25:26-30 My '80.

Reconstructionist rabbis issue guidelines. Recon 46:28-30 Mr '80.

Rabbi Schindler's call to convert: Are we ready? R.P. Jacobs. J Reform Jud 27:30-9 Sp '80.

Another look at conversion. J.J. Cohen. Forum No. 37:117-22 Sp '80.

Letter. L. Epstein. Con Jud 33:96 Sp '80.

RRA guidelines on conversion. Cong Mo 47:16-17 Ja '80.

Special issue Cong Mo 46: N '79.

Special issue: Gerut and the Conservative Movement. Con Jud 33, Fall '79.

Intermarriage and the proselyte: a Jewish view. M.A. Moskowitz. Jud 28;423-33 Fall '79.

Cum nimis absurdum and the conversion of the Jews. D. Berger. Jew Q R 70:41-9 Jl '79.

Conversion as an obstacle course. T. Friedman. Con Jud 32:96-100 Sum '79.

CONVERSION

Conversion. (A. Schindler) Letters. S.M. Cohen; B. Levin. Moment 4:3+ Je '79.

Converting the Gentiles. P.L. Berger. Commentary 67:35-9 My '79.

The issue is conversion. Moment 4:17-19 Mr '79.

Making it in Judaism. S. Morton. Mid 25:13-23 Mr '79.

Comment. (A. Schindler) L. Pfeffer; H. Schulweis; D. Schwartz. Moment 4:25-8 Mr '79.

A conversion at Santa Cruz, California, 1877. ed G.J. Fogelson. West States Jew Hist Q 11:139-44 Ja '79.

Conversion according to Halakha. T. Weiss-Rosmarin. Editorial. Jew Spec 43:3-5 W '78.

Comments: the proposal for a "neutral Beis Din." J.D. Bleich. Jew Life 2:6-10 Fall/W '77-'78.

Rabbis in Israel: a compromise? A. Soloff. Jew Fron 45:24-6 F '78.

A necessary paradox: catechesis and evangelism, nurture, and conversion III. J. Westerholl III. Symposium. Rel Ed 73:409-16 Jl/Ag '78.

Twice converted. K. Jones. Jew Spec 43:41-4 Sum '78.

News and comments: "Peace now" vs. settlements; Soldier of misfortune; Medical services in Lebanon; Lebanese baby named Israela; Demography and strategy; Law on conversion; labor strikes again; Century-old-immigrant; Heart-transplant patient; First Bedouin teachers; Filmmaking in Israel; Saudis bar blacks. Had Mag 59:26-9 My '78.

Israel's converts to Judaism. J.E. Gordon. Jew Spec 42:33-4 W '77.

Letter: Conversion. S. Handelman. Moment 2:6-8 O '77.

Survey of recent Halakhic periodical literature. J.D. Bleich. Trad 16:79-91 Fall '79.

New approach to conversion. J. Derby. Un Syn Rev 30:6-7+ Sum '77.

CONVERSION

The case against "quickie conversions." R.N. Levy. cond Jew Digest 22:10-15 My '77.

Conversion to Judaism. W.J. Hurwitz. Jew Spec 41:31-5 Sum '76.

American Jewry -- the ever-dying people. M. Sklare. Address. Adapt. Mid 22:17-27 Je/Jl '76.

Are you Jewish? (In America) E. Frisbie. Had Mag 57:17+ My '76.

Conversion and acceptance. M. Falconer. Had Mag 57:16+ My '76.

It begins with love. (in Israel) J.C. Jacobson. Had Mag 57:17+ My '76.

Conversion with yourself. A remarkable letter from Johann Heinrich Pestalozzi. A.A. Chiel. Rel Ed 71:217-18 Mr/Ap '76.

How does one join the Jewish people? M. Hurvitz. Recon 42:17-23 Ja '76.

The advisability of seeking converts. G. Kollin. Jud 24:49-57 W '75.

A Christian seeks conversion to Judaism - 1788. Amer Jew Arc 27:246 N '75.

Let's encourage converts. G. Kollin. Keeping Posted 21:8j+ N '75.

A missionary religion? B.J. Bamberger. Keeping Posted 21:3-7 N '75.

Who is a Jew - round III. S. Oren. Mid 21:38-44 Je/Jl '75.

Black Jews: a halakhic perspective. J.D. Bleich. Trad 15:48-79 Sp-Sum '75.

Conversion and Conservative Judaism. A.J. Yuter. Letter. Jew Spec 40:77-8 Ap '75.

The peculiar people and the Jews. A. Shankman. Amer Jew Hist Q 64:224-35 Mr '75.

On inter-racial conversion. E.N. Lear. Recon 40:22-9 D '74.

Conversion "According to Halakhah" - what is it? E. Berkovits. Jud 23:467-78 Fall '74.

CONVERSION

On conversion. W.G. Plaut. Letter. Cong bi-W 41:23 N 8 '74.

Danny Bernstein's shiksa. M.J. Routtenberg. cond Jew Digest 20:33-7 O '74.

Where did all the young Jews go? R. Larson. cond Jew Digest 20:62-5 O '74.

Rabin's bid for a bigger cabinet: Religious Party split on conversions plan. Jew Ob 23:16 S 6 '74.

American Jews and the Protestant community. G.S. Strober. Mid 20:47-66 Ag/S '74.

Belonging. F. Buckvar. cond Jew Digest 19:23-8 Ag '74.

Alienation and the Jewish Jesus freaks. M. Adler. Jud 23:287-97 Sum '74.

Conversion to Judaism. T. Weiss-Rosmarin. Editorial. Jew Spec 39:78-80 Sum '74.

The response of Jewish family service to the issue of conversion and intermarriage. A. Weinberg. J Jew Com Ser 50:340-8 Sum '74.

Who is a Jew: who decides? N. Levine. Address. Cong bi-W 41:20-1 Ap 19 '74.

Who is a Jew: who decides? H. Levine. Address. Cong bi-W 41:17-18 Ap 19 '74.

Who is a Jew: who decides? A. Anker. Address. Cong bi-W 41:16-17 Ap 19 '74.

Who is a Jew: who decides? C. Leibman. Address. Cong bi-W 41:18-19 Ap 19 '74.

Who is a Jew? J.J. Goldberg. Jew Fron 41:44-7 Mr '74.

Conversions. J.J. Petuchowski. Letter. Trad 14:138-9 Sp '74.

Conversion and Conservative Judaism. T. Friedman. Con Jud 28:21-9 Sp "74.

Converting because of marriage motives. M.S. Goodblatt. Con Jud 28:30-40 Sp '74.

CONVERSION

Mixed marriages pledge by Goren. Jew Ob 22:15 Ag 10 '73.

Conversion in Jewish law. S. Riskin. Trad 14:29-42 Fall '73.

Wishful thinking. D.M. Eichhorn. Jew Spec 38:10-11 Je '73.

Ger toshav and mixed marriage. A.D. Fisher. Recon 39:22-6 My '73.

Conversion, love and togetherness. E.H. Friedman. Recon 39:13-21 My '73.

Wanted: Jewish missionaries. A.S. Maller. Jew Spec 38;17-18 Ap '73.

What has happened to the converts? I.S. Borvick. Jew Life 40;11-16 Ja '73.

CONVERTS

Deep in the heart: a Yom Kippur in Texas. J.J. Davidson. Address. J Reform Jud 29;21-4 W '82.

Halfway between. C. Yair. Forum Nos. 46-47:237-44 Fall/W '82.

Definitions. F. Gerson. Letter on A.H. Gerson's essay. Mid 28:63 N '82.

Basketball and conversions. S. Spiegler. J Jew Com Ser 59;194-5 W '82.

My road to Judaism. N.T. Frey. Jew Spec 47;50-2 Sum '82.

Letter from Ocean Springs. E. O'Sullivan. Jew Mo 96:13-14 My '82.

Arnold Schoenberg's Judaism. W. Rimber. Mid 28:43-5 Ap '82.

Jews for Jesus: Mandelstam, Pasternak, Weil. M. Syrkin. cond Jew Digest 27:35-44 mr '82.

From schochet to anglican bishop of Jerusalem. L.L. Rabinowitz. cond Jew Digest 27:32-3 N '81.

A convert's road to prayer. G. Berkeley. Response 13:138-42 Fall W '81.

A perspective on intermarriage and conversion. L. Simon. Recon 46:7-14 F '81.

CONVERTS

Marcia's minyan. R.S. Wolk. Had Mag 62:30-2 Je-Jl '81.

Conversion to Judaism: an analysis of family matters. S. Huberman. Jud 30:312-21 Sum '81.

Becoming Jewish; a convert's story. C. Head. il Shraga Weil. Nat Jew Mo 95:4-5+ Mr '81.

Jews by choice. E.C. Fenig; J. Bush. Letters. Moment 6:5+ S '81.

Jacob A. Riis: christian friend or missionary foe? Two Jewish views. J.S. Gurock. Amer Jew Hist 71:29-47 S '81.

Communication. J.A. Edelheit. J Reform Jud 28:101-2 Sp '81.

Can religion be a test of sanity? A.A. Chiel. cond Jew Digest 26:72-80 ja '81.

My way to Judaism. N. Wingerson. Jew Spec 45:46-8 W '80.

Accepting non-Jews as members of the synagogue. J.S. Edelheit; A. Meth. J Reform Jud 24:87-92 Sum '80.

Converting to Judaism. D.F. Freidman. Jew Spec 45:43-4 Sp '80.

Jews by choice: forum on converts. cond Jew Digest 25:42-51 Ja '80.

Converts. J.E. Gordon. Letter. Jew Spec 44:63 W '79.

Is there anything after conversion? L. Byard. Recon 45:21-5 D '79.

Is there anything after conversion? A.S. Maller. Recon 45:25-30 D '79.

Jew -- not convert. S.A. Shachar. Moment 5:63-4 D '79.

Discussion: American Jewish Congress conference on conversion. D. Syme. Cong Mo 46:15-16 N '79.

Discussion: American Jewish Congress conference on conversion. S. Aimmerman. Cong Mo 46:17-18 N '79.

Discussion: American Jewish Congress conference on conversion. S. Seltzer. Cong Mo 46:18-19 N '79.

CONVERTS

Some demographic and cultural aspects of the new proselytism. M.F. Berbit. Cong Mo 46:8-12 N '79.

Conversion in the history of Jewish thought. A.J. Lelyveld. Cong Mo 46:4-8 N '79.

A star-crossed childhood. R. Abelson. Moment 4:59-61+ O '79.

I am a convert. N. Milo-Grob. Letter. Jew Spec 44:62-3 Sum '79.

Jews by choice. A discussion with converts. Moment 4:29-35 Mr '79.

Jewish assertiveness in combating missionaries. R.J. Birnholz. cond Jew Digest 24:18-23 N '78.

Jewish youth in transit. D.R. La Magdaleine. Cong Mo 45:8-9 Je '78.

Did the Berbers convert to Judaism? J.R. Rosenbloom. J Reform Jud 25:17-21 Sum '78.

Being a Jew may be hard -- becoming one is harder still. K. Jones. Moment 2:19-22 My '77.

Baseball's most valuable player and Judaism. M. Elkin. cond Jew Digest 23:18-19 F '78.

Are your children immune from missionaries? S.S. Jacobs. cond Jew Digest 23:10-12 D '77.

"Heavenly deception" Rev. Moon's hard sell. D. Silverberg. Present Tense 4:49-56 Autumn '76.

Almost certainly Jewish! Letters. Israel Mowshowitz; Paul Kaplowitz; Helen Jones. Present Tense 4:5-6+ Autumn '76.

Let us welcome converts. Letter. S. Stern. Jew Spec 41:76 Fall '76.

Discovering Judaism. S. Rishe. Jew Spec 41:59-60 Fall '76.

Hebrew Christianity. D.M. Eichhorn. Jew Spec 41:33-5 Fall '76.

My father and I; confessons of a convert's son. J. Silverlight. Present Tense 3:52-6 Sum '76.

CONVERTS

From Mississippi to Safad. M. Zimmerman. cond <u>Jew</u> <u>Digest</u> 21:35-7 My '76.

News and comments: Dove gets government job; A taxing situation; Mounting protests; Plastic bag Olympics; Civil guard recruits; Arms for the first century; Home-sick horses; Young convert, old Rabbi. <u>Had</u> <u>Mag</u> 57:35-8 Ap '76.

Why I want to attend the Reconstructionist rabbinical college. S. Edwards. <u>Recon</u> 42:14-19 Mr '76.

An aleph for the Russian general. M.B.H. Hillel. <u>Had</u> <u>Mag</u> 57:12 Ja '76.

Some persons who adopted Judaism. <u>Keeping</u> <u>Posted</u> 21:23 N '75.

A Jew by choice. M. Falconer. <u>Keeping</u> <u>Posted</u> 21:21-3 N '75.

Plain talk on small town Jews. (Winona, Minnesota) S.K. Hull. cond <u>Jew</u> <u>Digest</u> 20:73-4 Ag '75.

To welcome new Jews. A.S. Maller. cond <u>Jew</u> <u>Digest</u> 20:34-6 Ag '75.

Judaism despite Christianity. R. Horwitz. <u>Jud</u> 24:306-18 Sum '75.

A Jewish mission to the Gentiles. A. Maller. cond <u>Jew</u> <u>Digest</u> 20:72 My '75.

What's in a (Jewish) name? R.J. Marx. adapt. <u>Jew</u> <u>Digest</u> 20:28 Ap '75.

The origin of America's black Jews. B. Felton. cond <u>Jew</u> <u>Digest</u> 20:12-16 N '74.

Avram Uri Kovner: a search. S.M. Ginsburg. Excerpt his Meshumadim in tsarischen Rusland. <u>Jud</u> 23:346-56 Sum '74.

Conversion and Jewish law. T. Weiss-Rosmarin. Editorial. <u>Jew</u> <u>Spec</u> 39;5-6 Fall '74.

Flashback. D. Cusenberry. cond <u>Jew</u> <u>Digest</u> 19:60-5 Ap '74.

Flashback. D. Cusenberry. <u>Recon</u> 39:27-32 D '73.

The first Sabbath. M. Falconer. <u>Recon</u> 39:22-6 D '73.

CONVERTS

The Jesus Jew. N.B. Mirsky. Recon 39:11-16 D '73.

Jews and Jesus freaks. A. Ungar. Recon 39:7-11 D '73.

Happy birthday, world. S. Avidor-Hacohen. Israel 5:14+ S '73.

The Jewish bishops. A.A. Chiel. cond Jew Digest 18:71-3 Je '73.

On Christian evangelism. Yowa. Jew Spec 38:20-1 My '73.

Going home. J.B. Mitchell. cond Jew Digest 18:39-42 My '73.

The universalism of the chosen people. H. Greenberg. Mid 19:38-65 Mr '73.

The proselytes. M.S. Shapiro. Jew Digest 18:81 F '73.

CULTS

On cults. Keeping kids out and getting them out. S. Spiegler. J Jew Com Ser 59:192-3 W '82.

Cult groups in Israel. R. Medroff. cond Jew Digest 28:52-5 N '82.

Watch out for the way. A.M. Schwartz. ADL Bull 39:11-13 O '82.

Jews among evangelists in Los Angeles. J. Gutwirth. Jew J Soc 24:39-55 Je '82.

Awaiting the Verdict on Recruitment. Richard Delgado. Center Magazine, March/April 1982.

Oddments. T. Weiss-Rosmarin. Editorial. Jew Spec 46:7-8; 10+ O '81.

Jews, cults and apostates. A.S. Maller. Jud 30:306-11 Sum '81. Reprint Jew Digest 27:3-9 S '81.

Identity status of Jewish youth pre- and post-cult involvement. Address. I.B. Gitelson; E.J. Reed. J Jew Com Ser 57:312-20 '81.

Probing the cults. S.J. Spero. Jew Spec 45:31-6 W '80.

The call of strange cults. G. Kollin. cond Jew Digest 26:25-32 O '80.

CULTS

Community responses to the proselytization of Jews. N. Isser; L.L. Schwartz. J Jew Com Ser 57:63-72 Fall '80.

The contemporary penitent personality: diagnostic, treatment, and ethical considerations with a particular type of religious patient. M.H. Spero. J Psychology and Jud 4:133-91 Sp '80.

Headlines & footnotes: Cults, religious needs and mind control. P. Cushman; L.S. Moses. Nat Jew Mo 94:4+ My '80.

The cults and the law. J.B. Robison; B. Steyer; M.D. Stern. Pat Prej 14:3-14 Ap '80.

Cults. Letters. E. Deitz; J. Robins; L. Zakim; H.L. Scales. Nat Jew Mo 95:58+ Mr '80.

Headlines & footnotes: The cult problem is a fake! R.I. Israel. Nat Jew Mo 94:34+ Ja '80.

Our gifted teens and the cults. S. Andron. Ped Rep 31:37-8 Fall '79.

B'nai B'rith confronts the cults. C. Neff. Nat Jew Mo 94:23-5 N '79.

The most dangerous cult. T. Weiss-Rosmarin. Jew Spec 44:4-5 Sum '79.

The challenge of the new secular religions. H.M. Schulweis. Con Jud 32:3-15 Sum '79.

The politics of Jonestown. M. Decter. Commentary 67:29-34 Ap '79.

New cults - why now? T. Shanker. ADL Bull 36;13-14 Mr/Ap '79.

Infiltrating "the Jews for Jesus." R.A. Cohen. Interview. cond Jew Digest 24:8-12 F '79.

Cult encounters. M. Appell. cond Jew Digest 24:16-25 F '79.

Maharishi U. Learning to levitate in Fairfield, Iowa. L. Tabak. il Moment 4:26-32 Ja-J '79.

Cult encounters. H.A. Simon. Letter. Moment 4:3 Ja-F '79.

The fruits of fanaticism. Editorial. Recon 44:3-4 Ja '79.

CULTS

In search of Hasidim. P. Epstein. Excerpt. Shefa 2:55-71 No. 1 '79.

A note on family rights, cults, and the law. L.L. Schwartz. J Jew Com Ser 55:194-8 W '78.

Cult encounters. M. Appell. Moment 4:19-24 N '78.

Teaching the "cults.' H. & M. Silberman. Letter. Jew Spec 43:57-8 Fall '78.

The public and private agenda in Jewish education. H.M. Schulweis. Ped Rep 30:2-6 Fall '78.

Letter to the editor. B.Z. Kogen. Jew Ed 46:48 Fall '78.

Cults and the vulnerability of Jewish youth. L.L. Schwartz. Jew Ed 46: 23-6+ Sum '78.

Christian missionaries and a Jewish response. B. Brickner. cond Jew Digest 23:10-19 Sum '78.

The new religious cults and the Jewish community. M.R. Rudin. Address. Symposium: Religious education and spiritual quest. Rel Ed 73:350-60 My/Je '78.

From Gurus to Gemara; Women return to tradition. R. Furstenberg. il Had Mag 59:14-15+ Ja '78.

Deprogramming: an exchange of letters. W. Goldberg, et al. Amer Zion 68:34-8 O '77.

The rise of a new polytheism. B. Hargrove. Address. Rel Ed 72:459-72 S/O '77.

Cults: some theoretical and practical perspectives. M.H. Spero. J Jew Com Ser 53:330-8 Sum '77.

Jews for Jesus. T. Weiss-Rosmarin. Letter. Moment 2:6 S '77.

The soul snatchers of Long Island. Can a Massapequa coffee house defend our children against a 12-acre estate in Stony Brook. S. Luxenberg. Photographs Bill Aron. Moment 2:7-10+ My '77.

Are we losing our children? M. Zeldner. Jew Fron 44:8-11 My '77.

CULTS

Deprogramming: a critical view. Y. Haramgaal. Am Zion 67:16-19
My-Je '77.

Religious cults: how serious a danger? T. Freedman. ADL Bull
34:1-2 Ap '77.

Kids in Cults: Why They Join, Why They Stay, Why They Leave.
Irvin Doress and Jack N. Porter. Reconciliation Association, 1977,
Brookline, Mass.

DEATH AND DYING

Fear of Personal Death: The Effects of Sex and Religious Belief.
Victor Florian; Dov Har-Even. Omega: Journal of Death and Dying,
vol. 14, no. 1, pp. 83-91, 198, 1983.

Dealing with tragedy in the classroom. B.J. Evans. cond Jew Digest
26:23-8 D '81.

Contemplating death. H.R. Nadich. Jew Spec 46:45 Sum '81.

Covenant faith for communal immortality. N.M. Landman. Recon
46:20-6 N '80.

Death education. J.B. Wolowelsky. Pedagogic Forum in Ped Rep
32:32-3 Fall '80.

Death, dying and grief: the past psychic barrier. E. Tarnoff. J Jew
Com Ser 56:181-9 W '79-'80.

The congregational need to mourn. M.M. Remson. J Reform Jud
27:91-2 W '80.

Hands. H.A. Addison. J Reform Jud 27;87-9 W '80.

Chronicle. Jew Jl Soc 21:181-6 D '79.

Death shall be defeated. A. Steinsaltz. Shefa 1:3-5 Ap '78.

God only knows. R. Nozick. Moment 3:17-18 Ja/F '78.

Communication: A.H. Friedland; D. Polish. CCARJ 24:108 W '77.

Halakhah as psychology: explicating the laws of mourning. M.H.L.
Spero. Trad 16:173-84 Fall '77.

DEATH AND DYING

Last words and deathbed scenes in rabbinic literature. A.J. Saldarini. Jew Q R 68:28-45 Jl '77.

O death, where is thy sting-a-ling-a-ling? L.H. Farber. Commentary 63:35-43 Je '77.

The right to die. The bio-ethical frontier: creating an agenda. L. Smolar. J Jew Com Ser 53:320-9 Sum '77.

Trying to define "death." D.C. Goldfarb. Keeping Posted 22:7-8+ N '76.

Jewish medical ethics. P.A. Bardfeld. Recon 42:7-12 S '76.

The Jewish way of death. I. Silverman. cond Jew Digest 22:55-61 S '76.

Toward new policies on Jewish funeral practices. Analysis, April '76, No. 56.

Remember us unto death. W.B. Silverman. cond Jew Digest 21:8-14 Ja '76.

Dignity lies in the struggle for life. Bleich. Sh'ma, Dec. 12, 1975.

When a life is no life - the right to die. Raskas. Sh'ma, Dec. 12, 1975.

The terminally ill; may we let them die. Levine. Sh'ma, Dec. 12, 1975.

To die with dignity. Editorial Recon 41:6 D '75.

The Halachic framework of mourning and bereavement and its implications for helping professions. R. Schindler. J Jew Com Ser 51:325-31 Sum '75.

Funerals aren't for children. P. Perlmutter. Jew Digest 20:31-4 Jl '75.

Children and death. M. Wessel. Un Syn Rev 28:6-7+ Sp '75.

How to tell children about death. M. Wessel. cond Jew Digest 20:48-52 S '75.

DEATH AND DYING

Hope and death. M. Greenberg. Address. adapt. il Ariel No
39:21-23+ '75.

Much ado about death. T. Weiss-Rosmarin. Editorial. Jew Spec
39:3-6 W '74.

The halachic framework of mourning and bereavement. Ruben
Schindler. Tradition, Fall 1975, Vol. 15, No. 3.

On death and dying. L.D. Lerner. Recon 40:11-15 F '74.

The problem of euthanasia. S. Rudikoff. Commentary 57;62-8 F '74.

Remembering us unto death. The rabbi confronts agonizing dilemmas.
W.B. Silverman CCARJ 21:41-68 Sp '74.

Updating the sanctity of life. M.L. Brill. Jew Spec 39:60-1 Sp '74.

Horace M. Kallen on death. H.M. Kallen. Jew Spec 39:59 Sp '74.

Man's power and limits in a technological age. S.E. Kariff. Jud
23:161-73 Sp '74.

A midrash on Jewish mourning. J.B. Wolowelsky. Jud 23:212-15 sp
'74.

The living and the dead: a cross-cultural perspective on Jewish
memorial observances. Joel S. Savishinsky; Howard Wimberley.
Jewish Social Studies 1974, 36, 3-4, Jul-Oct, 281-300.

Establishing criteria of death. J.D. Bleich. Trad 13:90-113 W '73.

Reflections on death. A.J. Heschel. Con Jud 28:3-9 Fall '73.

Water wings for the river of death. H.H. Zietlow. Rel Ed 68:476-82
Jl/Ag '73.

Euthanasia. B.L. Sherwin. cond Jew Digest 18:51-3 Ja '73.

DEMOGRAPHY

Diaspora population: past growth and present decline. R. Bachi.
Jerusalem Q No 22:3-16 W '82.

Westward, ho? Jew Digest 28:9 O '82.

DEMOGRAPHY

Jewish population figures. S. Spiegler. J Jew Com Ser 58:361-2 Sum '82.

American Jews: patterns of geographic distribution and change. W.N. Newman; P. Halvorson. Jews for Science and Study of Religion, Vol. 18, #2, 1979, pp. 183-193.

Demographic trends and Jewish survival. S.S. Lieberman; M. Weinfeld. cond Jew Digest 24:50-60 Mr '79.

The demographics of Jewish life in the U.S.; a presentation of 14th American Israel dialogue. H. Bienstock. Cong Mo 46:16 F/Mr '79.

The coming shrinkage of American Jewry. pt. 2. S.M. Cohen; B. Rosenberg. Excerpt their Issues in the Jewish experience. Jew Digest 24:17-24 Ja '79.

Recent patterns of Chicago Jewish residential mobility. Charles Jaret. Ethnicity, Vol. 6, No. 3, pp. 235-48, Sep. 1979.

An optimum population of a survivalist ethnic community: socio-demographic trends and group characteristics. Morton Weinfeld. McGill U, Montreal Quebec H3C 3G1. Conference: SSSP - Society for the Study of Social Problems. 1978.

The coming shrinkage of American Jewry. S.M. Cohen; B. Rosenberg. Excerpt their issues in the Jewish experience. pt 1. Jew Digest 24:3-9 D '78.

Demographic trends and Jewish survival. S.S. Lieberman; M. Weinfeld. Mid 24:9-19 N '78.

Updating the life cycle of the family. Journal of Marriage and the Family, XXXIX, No. 1, 1977, pp. 5-13.

The American Jewish population erosion. E. Bergman. Mid Winter '77.

Surviving the infertile years: the synagogue and the community. Mordechai Waxman. Analysis, No. 60, Nov-Dec 1976, pp. 9-12.

World overpopulation and Jewish underpopulation. Editorial. Recon 42:3-4 Ap '76.

World Jewish population 14,150,000. World Over 36:4 F 14 '76.

DEMOGRAPHY

A Jew is a Jew is a Jew? not in Canada. S. Spiegler. J Jew Com Ser 51:303 Sp '75.

Too many and too mighty... T. Weiss-Rosmarin. Jew Spec 40:15+ Sp '75.

"People plague" and "birth death." J.D. Spiro. Keeping Posted 20:8+ Ap '75.

Jews and population control. H.O. Schoenberg. Cong bi-W 41:16-17 D 6 '74.

No Jews, no Jewish identity. M. Himmelfarb. Address. cond Jew Digest 20:17-19 O '74.

Statistics anyone? S. Spiegler. J Jew Com Ser 50:271-2 Sp '74.

Estimating Jewish population distribution in U.S. metropolitan areas in 1970. I. Rosenwaike. Jew SS 36:106-17 Ap '74.

World Jewish population now more than 14 million. World Over 35:5 Ja 25 '74.

U.S. National Jewish Population Study. F. Masserik; A. Chenkin. American Jewish Year Book, 1973, Vol. 74, pp. 264-306.

Too smart to leave. W. Korey. Nat Jew Mo 88:38+ D '73.

The next 25 years. M. Louvish. cond Jew Digest 19:69-72 O '73.

Jewish population estimates. S. Spiegler. J Jew Com Ser 49:253-4 Sp '73.

Population rising to half a million? Jew Ob 22:13 Ap '73.

DIVORCE

Beineinu: The divorced-parent family in the synagogue community. B.K. Bundt. Con Jud 35:74-7 W '82.

Coming of age in remarried families: the Bar Mitzvah. L.H. Perlmutter. Address. J Jew Com Ser 59:58-65 Fall '82.

Conservative Judaism and the agunah. S.H. Schwarz. Con Jud 36:37-44 Fall '82.

DIVORCE

A note on phantom triads: family coalitions and religious observance after divorce. T.D. Marciano. Jew SS 44:315-22 Sum/Fall '82.

This month: Interview with Ida Nudel; Trouble in Guatemala; Last Jew in Harbin; One Sharansky square; Israel hot line; Ketuba problems; Comic book hero. Had Mag 63:28-9 Je-Jl '82.

Divorce. R. Seligman. Jid 28:35-7 Mr '82.

Brooklyn man ordered to give "get" to his Israeli wife. Jew Life 6:61-2 Sp/Sum '82.

One single Jew. S.P. Weinberg. cond Jew Digest 27:48-54 Ja '82.

Some implications for Jewish marriage philosophy for marital breakdown. Reuven P. Bulka. Pastoral Psychology, Winter 1981.

The divorced woman in I Cor 7:10-11. J. Murphy-O'Connor. J Bib Lit 100:601-1 D '81.

Special issue Keeping Posted 37: O '81.

Bar Mitzva when parents are no longer partners. E.H. Friedman. J Reform Jud 28;53-66 Sp '81.

The legal status of women in Israel. S.E. Shanoff. Cong Mo 48:9-12 Je '81.

New alternatives for Jewish family in transition. E. Lauter. cond Jew Digest 26:9-12 Mr '81.

Getting un-married: a model for divorce education. J.H. Spitzer. J Jew Com Ser 57:98-101 Fall '80.

Reconstructionist rabbinical association introduces "egalitarian" divorce. I. Eisenstein. Recon 47:28-9 Je '80.

Children of divorced parents households - some suggested guidelines for school or synagogue. S. Seltzer. Program Perspectives, UAHC, March 1980.

The family in transition: a search for new answers. E. Lauter. Recon 45:13-17 Ja '80.

Letter to the editor. N.B. Shapiro. Reply B. Greenberg. Lilith 1:46 F/W '77/'78.

DIVORCE

The Beth Din in action. S. Fields. cond Jew Digest 23:57-9 F '78.

Divorce and the Jewish woman: a family agency approach. J Lang. Address. J Jew Com Ser 54:220-8 Sp '78.

Divorce in Jewish Life and tradition, a mini-course. P. Benson; S. Bissell. Alternative in Religious Education, 1977, 17 pp. (with leader guide).

Divorce. Letter J. Dick. Response I.H. Haut. Trad 16:191-4 Fall '77.

The rabbi and divorce. E.F. Lipman. CCARJ 24:29-34 Autumn '77.

Jewish divorce law. B. Greenberg. Lilith 1:26-9 Sp/Sum '77.

A problem in Jewish divorce law: an analysis and some suggestions. I.H. Haut. Trad 16:29-49 Sp '77.

Jewish divorce in American courts. Bernard J. Meislin. Journal of Family Law, 1977-78, 16, 1, 19-35.

Family disintegration and the role of the paraprofessional in the synagogue. A.D. Sorosky. Recon 42:18-28 D '76.

To be Jewish and divorced in Columbus, Ohio. Letter. M.L. Raphael. Jew Spec 41:58-60 W '76.

Divorce: the problem and the challenge. R.P. Bulka. Trad 16:127-33 Sum '76.

Annulment of marriage within the context of the Get. A. Rakeffet-Rothkoff. Trad 15:173-85 Sp-Sum '75.

Rap session. J. Fisher. Keeping Posted 20:21 Ap '75.

Marriage - a small technicality. S. Spiegler. J Jew Com Ser 50:272 Sp '74.

The duty of the synagogue to its widows and divorcees. S. Glustrom. Un Syn Rev 26:14-15 Sp '73.

EDUCATION

Family education: The joy of Shabbat; Fourth-grade family makhon; Family education days; Early childhood center for Jewish immigrant children. Ped Rep 33:4-5 My '82.

Jew education: problems, prospects and the challenge. A.I. Schiff. Editorial. Jew Ed 49:2-8 W '81; cond Jew Digest 27:48-54 Ap '82.

Working daughters. S.S. Weinberg. Reprint. ' cond Jew Digest 27:51-8 Mr '82.

Report on research and activities, 1981-1982, No. 6. Hebrew Univ. Jerusalem (Israel). School of Education; National Council of Jewish Women. New York, N.Y. Research Inst. for Innovation in Education. May 1982, 86p.

On the making of Jews. W.I. Ackerman. Jud 30:87-95 W '81.

A cooperative program between a Jewish day school and a Jewish family agency. J.L. Dolins; W.M. Greene; G.P. Lissek. Jew Ed 49:14-22 W '81.

Impact of Jewish education on Jewish identification in a group of adolescents. J. Sigal. Jew SS 43:229-36 Sum/Fall '81.

Who are our children? (Analysis of an informal questionnaire.) H.M. Cohen. Ped Forum in Ped Rep 32:31-3 S '81.

I Q on trial. N. Glazer. Commentary 71:51-9 Je '81.

A study of interaction effects of school and home environments on students of varying race/ethnicity, class, and gender. Final report. Volume II: ethnographies of five racial/ethnic groups. John D. Herzog; and others. TDR Association, Inc., Newton, Mass. Dec 1981, 538p.

Educational change and its effect on culturally disadvantaged population: a case study, Israel. Moshe Papo. 1981, 29p.

Current trends in Jewish communal education. G. Pollak; B. Efron. Reprint. Ped Rep 31:19 W /80.

A look into the eighties. G. Pollak. Curriculum Newsletter in Ped Rep 31:31-2 W '80.

Jewish family life education and the Orthodox day school. R.J. Levin; K.A. Bruss. J Jew Com Ser 57:94-7 Fall '80.

EDUCATION

Better education for fewer children. A.I. Schiff. Editorial. <u>Jew Ed</u> 48;2-3 Sum '80.

Jewish continuity through Jewish education: a human resource imperative. A.I. Schiff. <u>Jew Ed</u> 48:5-11+ Sum '80.

250,000 children of our fathers. I. Kegler. <u>Mid</u> 26:34-7 Ja '80.

In pursuit of quality: two departures in Jewish education. The home as a Hebrew school. R. Milch. <u>Moment</u> 4:53-7 Je '79.

The diagnosis and treatment of underachievement. Michael Goodstein. B'nai B'rith, Wahsington, D.C. Career and Counseling Services. Counselor's Information Service, Vol, 34, No. 4, Suppl. 1, Dec 1979.

One family's frustration. B. Glasser. <u>Moment</u> 3:18-24 Autumn '78.

Parents and children go to nursery school. B. Chankin. <u>Ped Rep</u> 30:27 Fall '78.

The public and private agenda in Jewish education. H.M. Schulweis. <u>Ped Rep</u> 30:2-6 Fall '78.

Helping the parent to be a parent: a new role for the yeshiva day school. Y. Feitman. <u>Ped Rep</u> 30:25-6 Fall '78.

To invent is to understand: creative aspects and perspectives of Jean Piaget's new discipline. J.F. Emling. <u>Rel Ed</u> 73:551-68 O '78.

Facing the future of Jewish education. E.B. Borowitz. <u>Jew Ed</u> 45:33-40 Sp '77.

The day school: the 'life school.' M. Siegel. <u>Un Syn Rev</u> 29:12-13 Ap '77.

Multicultural education: a functional bibliography for teachers. Milton J. Gold, Ed.; Carl A. Grant, Ed. Nebraska Univ., Omaha. Center for Urban Education. 1977, 46p.

What parents want from the Jewish education of their children. A.'A. Lasker. <u>J Jew Com Ser</u> 52:393-403 Sum '76.

Bibliographic index of American Ethnic groups, volume I and volume II. Thomas Sowell. Urban Inst., Washington, D.C. 1976, 681p.

EDUCATION

The source of our home. I. Eisenstein. Address. Recon 41:7-10 S '75.

Home and school: the great divide. B. Barwell. Jew Ob 24:18 N 21 '75.

The impact of Jewish education on relgious identification and practice. Steven Martin Cohen. Jewish Social Studies 1974, 36, 3-4, Jul-Oct, 316-326.

Extension of family agency services to a Hebrew day school. C. Himmelfarb. J Jew Com Ser 49:313-17 Sum '73.

Sexism, drop-outs and Jewish federations. A.S. Maller. Jew Fron 40:29-31 S '73.

SPECIAL EDUCATION - CHILDREN

H. Faigel's article "Jewish education for the learning disabled." E. Normand. Letter. Moment 4:4+ Mr '79.

Every tenth child. Jewish education for the learning disabled. H. Faigel. Moment 4:60-2 D '78.

Social agency guardianship. L.D. Fisher; M. Najberg; D. Soyer. Address. J Jew Com Ser 54:54-61 Fall '77.

New approach to retarded children (Akim). Address. Extract. N. Rafael. Jew Ob 24:10 My 23 '75.

Praise for work among retarded (Akim). Jew Ob 24:18 My 9 '75.

The Jewish learning disabled child; perspective on a growing problem. H.A. Greenberg. Con Jud 28;41-8 Sp '74.

Mental retardation and religious education. L. Bogardus. Rel Ed 68:260-2 Mr/Ap '73.

ETHICS

An I for an I. H. Schulweis. Moment 6:21-4 D '80.

Creating life. R.F. Address. Jew Spec 45:26-7 Sum '80.

Rediscovering Jewish ethics. E.H. Yoffie. Jew Spec 45:45-7 Sum '80.

ETHICS

Jewish ethics in action. N. Lamm. Excerpt his Man in society. Jew Heritage 15:25-9 Sum/Fall '73.

The a priori component of bioethics. J.D. Bleich. Jew Life 3:71-9 Sum/Fall '78.

Test-tube babies. D.C. Gross; B. Postal. cond Jew Digest 24:66-70 D '78.

Euthanasia: a classical ethical problem in a modern context. A. Bar-Zev. Recon 44: 7-16 Ja '79.

ETHNICITY

Are we ready for the new Jewish community? J.A. Edelheit. J Reform Jud 29:14-20 W '82.

On becoming Jewish. A. Potok; A. Landa. Moment 5:16-20+ S '80.

The new ethnicity, religious survival, and Jewish identity: the "Judaisms" of our newest members. D. Ellenson. Address. J Reform Jud 26;47-60 Sp '79.

Class, kinship, and ethnicity: patterns of Jewish upward mobility in Pittsburgh, Pennsylvania. Myrna Silverman. Urban Anthropology, 1978, 7, 1, Spring, 25-43.

The new ethnicity. M. Novak. cond Jew Digest 20:57 Mr '75.

Is there a "Jewish look"? W. Sneader. cond Jew Digest 20:54-5 F '75.

A path toward Jewish unity. D. Polish. Address. Recon 40:7-14 Ja '75.

Taboo or not taboo? M.S. Shapiro. Jew Digest 19:81 Ap '74.

FAMILY EDUCATION, JEWISH

Adult education: teaching aleph-bet to adults. Workshop on Jewish parenting. Ped Rep 33:16 My '82.

Parents go to school. G. Weiss. Ped Rep 32:33-4 W '81.

Family Education. Robin Eisenberg. Compass Fall 1981.

FAMILY EDUCATION, JEWISH

Open forum: teaching Conservative Judaism and the Jewish family. S. Schafler. Con Jud 33:73-8 Fall '79.

A family systems approach to religious education and development. S.M. Natale. Rel Ed 74:245-53 My-Je '79.

Some Jewish aspects of filial piety-Kibbud av ve-em. S. Teitelbaum. J Reform Jud 17-24 Fall '78.

The United Synagogue family education program. M. Siegel. Ped Rep 30:11-12 Fall '78.

Jewish family education. D.P. Elkins. Ped Rep 30:7-10 Fall '78.

Torah for life. D. Isaacs. Ped Rep 30:34 Fall '78.

Bureau sets tone for raising the status of family education. M. Samber. Ped Rep 30;12-13 Fall '78.

Program in Jewish family life education. comp M. Rockowitz. Ped Rep 28:10-34 Sp '77.

Family education: a new frontier? I. Toubin. Ped Rep 28:2-3 Sp '77.

Jewish family education. B. Reisman. Ped Rep 28:4-10 Sp '77.

Adult, family, and parent education. R. Kronish; M. Herman; S. Lowenstein. Ped Rep 27:3-4 W '76.

The family cluster; a new model for Jewish education. D.P. Elkins. Un Syn Rev 28:18-19+ Sp-Sum '76.

An experience in training staff for Jewish family life education. J. Bronstein. Address. J Jew Com Ser 52:210-15 W '75.

Total family education. Directions and problems. E.D. Kiner. CCARJ 22:61-70 W '75.

Parent, adult and family education. Congregation Beth Israel, San Diego, California; Hebrew Institute of Pittsburgh, Pittsburgh, Pennsylvania; Park Synagogue Religious School, Cleveland Heights, Ohio; United Synagogue of America, New York (city). Ped Rep 25:12 W '74.

Family cluster education. M.M. Sawin. Rel Ed 68:275-6 Mr/Ap '73.

FAMILY LIFE, JEWISH

Comment: The Jewish family: authority and tradition in modern perspective. M.R. Startz. Address. J Jew Com Ser 59:144-7 W '82.

The Jewish family in crisis. Adapt Jew Digest 28:21 D '82.

"Send me my husband who is in New York City": husband desertion in the American Jewish immigrant community, 1900-1926. R.S. Friedman. Jew SS 44:1-18 W '82.

Another look at the diagnosis and treatment of Orthodox Jewish family problems. M. Wikler. J Psychology and Jud 7:42-54 Fall/W '82.

New pockets of Jewish energy: A study of adults who found their way back to Judaism. AJC, Nov 1982.

The Bar Mitzvah as an experience in family growth. S. Blitstein. J Jew Com Ser 59:45-57 Fall '82.

The Jewish family: realities and prospects. R.P. Bulka. Jew Life 6:25-34 Sp/Sum '82.

"Buruch Ha'Shem, not so good": some concerns of Jewish women. J. Wolf. Jew Life 6:47-53 Sp/Sum '82.

Family life education in an urban synagogue. V. Kurtz. Rel Ed 77:321-35 My-Je '82.

The Jewish family. Outlook, Women's League, Sp. 1982.

Youth education as problematizing political forms. K. Scott. Rel Ed 77:197-210 Mr-Ap '82.

Making it in middle age. Robey Bryant. J American Demographics, Feb., 1982.

The American Jewish family today. Steven M. Cohen. American Jewish Year Book, 1982. A.J.C., J.P.S., New York.

Family as a Jewish value. Newsletter-National Jewish Family Center, AJC, Manh. 1982.

The Jewish family: a perspective. Newsletter-AJC, July 1982.

FAMILY LIFE, JEWISH

The effect of religion on women's rights and family issues. Glenna D. Spitze; Joan Huber. State U New York, Albany. Conference: ASA (American Sociological Association). 1982.

Religious loyalties in clinical work: a contextual view. B. Krasner. J Jew Com Ser 58:108-14 W '81-2.

Comment on: direct treatment of children in the family and children's agency. J.L. Taylor. Address. J Jew Com Ser 47:142-4 W '80-1.

Direct treatment of children in the family and children's agency: toward an integrated practice. J.M. Goldsmith; J. Lang. Address. J Jew Com Ser 47:131-41 W '80-1.

Families at mid-life. Fran Blevey. CJF-General Assembly, Nov. 1981.

Dynamics of the Soviet Jewish family. Phyllis Hulewat. J Jew Com Ser Fall 1981.

The changing role of Jewish women: implications for family, social work agency and social work practice. D.C. Pressma. Address. J Jew Com Ser 58:67-75 Fall '81.

Echoes. W. Kaelter. J Reform Jud 28:47-9 Sum '81.

What is the Jewish 'family' today? A.S. Maller. cond Jew Digest 26:16-21 Sum '81.

A Jewish approach. D. Waysman. Israel Scene 24 S '81.

Jewish family: a woman alone. Israel Scene 21-2 S '81.

The family: a central focus for practice. Ann Hartman. Social Work January 1981.

Kinship marriage and the family. Michael Verdon. American Journal of Sociology, January 1981.

Family life, Jewish. Special issue. Recon 46: Ja '81.

The Jewish family today. A.S. Maller. Recon 46:7-12 Ja '81.

Special child advocates: a volunteer court program. Michael Blady. Children Today, vol. 10, No. 3, pp. 2-6. May-Jun 1981.

FAMILY LIFE, JEWISH

Childspacing among the Jews of Middletown, Connecticut. Jerrold Mirotznik; Jacob Jay Lindenthal. Contemporary Jewry 1980, 5, 1, Spring-Summer, 64-70.

The joy of children. R. Mecklenburer. Letter. Jew Spec 45:61-2 W '80.

Guest comments: a rabbi writes to his congregants. J.D. Bleich. Jew Life 4:8-10 Fall '80.

Dynamics of communal cooperation. O.B. Rand. Jew Ed 48:4-8+ Fall '80.

Family day care in the United States: family day care systems. Final report of the national day care home study. Volume 5. Janet Grasso; Steven Fosburg. Abt. Associations, Inc., Cambridge, Mass.; Center for Systems and Program Development, Inc., Washington, D.C.; SRI International, Menlo Park, Calif. 1 Aug 1980, 185p.

The changing Jewish family and the crisis of values: the role and impact of the professional in Jewish communal services. J Lang. J Jew Com Ser 56:301-5 Sum '80.

The needs of the middle years - a new area of exploration. Institute for Jewish Policy Planning and Research, Synagogue Council of America, June 1980.

The family, feminism and religious education. K. Scott. Rel Ed 75:327-41 My-Je '80.

Family enrichment - the challenge which unites us. M. Sawin. Rel Ed 75:342-53 My-Je '80.

The family in transition: a search for new answers. E. Lauter. Recon 45:13-16 Ja 1980.

Saving the Jewish family. E. Gilbson. Jew Spec 44:34-7 W '79.

The contemporary family and the responsibilities of the social worker in direct practice. H.S. Strean. J Jew Com Ser 5:40-9 Fall '79.

The Jewish family and Jewish communal service: a crisis of values. B. Reisman. Address. J Jew Com Ser 56:35-9 Fall '79.

Can the women's movement save the Jewish family? G. Rosen. cond Jew Digest 24:10-16 Jl/Ag '79.

FAMILY LIFE, JEWISH

The Sabbath family. S. Shafton. Recon 45:17-22 Jl '79.

The family laws of Leviticus 18 in their setting. S.F. Bigger. J Bib Let 98:187-203 Je '79.

The Jewish family: an endangered species? G. Rosen. Address. J Jew Com Ser 55:345-52 Sum '79.

The centrality of the family in defining Jewish identity and identification. C.I. Waxman. J Jew Com Ser 55:353-9 Sum '79.

Assessing the effectiveness of a family life education program. E. Rosen; H. Benus. J Jew Com Ser 55:333-8 Sum '79.

Strengthening the Jewish family through clinical practice. S. Hofstein. J Jew Com Ser 55:375-81 Sum '79.

The impact of the women's movement on the Jewish family. G. Rosen. Jud 28:160-8 Sp '79.

Home in a kibbutz. Y.A. Gibson. Mid 25:24-9 My '79.

Merging to cultures: birth of a new Jewish family. Altman Cintron. Jewish Currents, January 1979, pp. 4-8.

National commission Jewish family life. S. Kamerman. AJC, 1979.

The Jewish family: past, present and future (a mini-course). P. Benson; J. Altschuler. Alternatives in Religious Education, 1979, 25p. (with leader guide).

How not to raise our children: theology and insecurity in childhood. R.R. Barr. Rel Ed 73:707-13 N-D '78.

A principal look at home-school cooperation. H.J. Campeas. Ped Rep 30:15-17 Fall '78.

The changing Orthodox Jewish family. G. Kranzler. Jew Life 3:23-36 Sum/Fall '78.

President's column. The Jewish family in crisis. D.M. Blumberg. Nat Jew Mo 92:22 Jl/Ag '78.

The effect of intensive Jewish education on adult Jewish life-styles. S. Ribner. Jew Ed 46:k6-12 Sp '78.

FAMILY LIFE, JEWISH

Perspectives on the Jewish single parent family. S. Hofstein.
Address. J Jew Com Ser 54:229-40 Sp '78.

Family theologizing and ritualizing: a study. Address. M. Hover.
Symposium: religious education and spiritual quest. Rel Ed 73:360-2
My/Je '78.

The rediscovery of the family. M. Glazer. Commentary 65:49-56 Mr
'78.

The agenda. D.M. Blumberg. Nat Jew Mo 92:19 F '78.

The president's column. B.S. Tannenbaum. Had Mag 59:2 Ja '78.

The worried Jewish parent's guide to cultural security. S., Dworkin.
Nat Jew Mo 92:7-9 Ja '78.

The changing family: its implications for early childhood centers.
N.L. Jacobs. Address. J Jew Com Ser 54:43-9 Fall '77.

Family change - nursery school response. H.I. Bogot. Address. J
Jew Com Ser 53:366-70 Sum '77.

Recollections of a rebbe's daughter. H.T. Rottenberg. Keeping Posted
23:16-18 N '77.

Remembering the new Amalekites. J. Pilch. Jew Fron 44:26-7 N
'77.

A family festival cluster. R.E. Murdock. Rel Ed 72:528-33 S-O '77.

Beating patriarchy at its own game. M.C. Schwartz. Lilith 1:37-40 W
'76/'77.

The Jewish prince: some continuities in traditional and contemporary
Jewish life. Zena Smith Blau. Contemporary Jewry 1977, 3, 2,
Spring-Summer, 54-71.

The Jewish family in early America. Herman Lantz; Mary O'Hara.
International Journal of Sociology of the Family 1977, 7, 2, July-Dec,
247-259.

Six years in isolation: a family's story. Leonard Nadler. Sh'ma, Vol.
7, No. 127, February 4, 1977, pp. 54-56.

FAMILY LIFE, JEWISH

The adaptable American Jewish family: an inconsistency in theory. G.S. Berman. Jewish Journal of Sociology, Vol. XVIII, No. 2, December 1976, pp. 5-16.

A family therapist's appraoch to working with an Orthodox Jewish clientele. S. Ostrov. Address. J Jew Com Ser 53:147-54 W '76.

The high price of "failure." M.C. Schwartz. Lilith 1:21+ Fall '76.

Reflections on family breakdown among Jewish families. B. Schlesinger. J Psychology and Jud 1:45-53 Fall '76.

Family mitzvah. M. Korman. Letter. Jew Spec 41:78 Sum '76.

Marriage and the family. Gerson D. Cohen. The Synagogue School, Vol. XXIV, No. 3-4, Spring 1976, pp. 4-19.

The impact of changing lifestyles on a family service agency. Address. S. Harris. J Jew Com Ser 52:249-58 Sp '76.

Grandparents rediscovered. D.G. Becker. J Jew Com Ser 52:240-8 Sp '76.

The adaptable American Jewish family: an inconsistency in theory. Gerald S. Berman. Jew J Soc 1976, 18, 1, Jun 5-16.

Ethnic differences in family attitudes towards psychotic manifestations, with implications for treatment programmes. Louise Wylan; Norbett L. Mintz. International Journal of Social Psychiatry 1976, 22, 2, Summer, 95-96.

Value perspectives on Jewish family life. Saul Berman. Social Casework 1976, 57, 6, Jun, 366-372.

The adaptable American Jewish family: an inconsistency in theory. G.S. Berman Jew J Soc 18:5-16 Je '76.

Family values and real life. Alvin L. Schorr. Social Casework 1976, 57, 6, Jun, 397-404.

Family life today. Social Casework, June 1976, Vol. 57, No. 6. A compendium of articles on general and Jewish family life.

The Jewish American prince. M.S. Kennedy. Moment 1:8+ My/Je '76.

FAMILY LIFE, JEWISH

Changing life styles. M.S. Shapiro. Address. pt.1. cond Jew Digest 21:15-21 Mr '76.

The rebbe's daughter. H.T. Rottenberg. cond Jew Digest 22:7-13 O '76.

Remodeling the new models. No gimmicks for holiness. R. Mills. CCARJ 22:31-3 W '75.

New families, old agencies. M.S. Shapiro. Jew Digest 20:79 Ag '75.

The Jewish family life institute: implementing priorities in the Jewish community center. G. Friedman. J Jew Com Ser 51:358-65 Sum '75.

Changing life styles, the Jewish family and the Jewish community. M.S. Shapiro. Address. Cong Mo 42:14-21 S '75.

The JCC's responsibility for the needs of the Jewish family. Gerald B. Bubis. J Jew Com Ser Spring 1975.

Family life council. D.P. Elkins. Recon 41:19-23 S '75.

The impact of family leisure time patterns on Jewish resident camping. S. Morton Altman. National Jewish Welfare Board, New York, N.Y. Apr 1975, 36p.

Are the Jews committing Jewish genocide? H.J. Roberts. cond Jew Digest 20:37-42 Mr '75.

Commitment and freedom: a paradox in service to the Jewish family. F. Berl. Address. J Jew Com Ser 51:151-61 W '74.

Finding grandparents. M.S. Shapiro. Jew Digest 20:80 D '74.

Endogenous Jewish genocide. H.J. Roberts. Recon 40:8-17 N '74.

The Jewish family in the days of Moses Maimonides. S.D. Gotein. Con Jud 29:25-35 Fall '74.

The changing family pattern and the persistence of tradition in the Jewish community: a case study. E. Mayer. J Jew Com Ser 51:82-9 Fall '74.

The Jewish family and religion. Benjamin Schlesinger. Journal of Comparative Family Studies 1974, 5, 2, AUT, 27-36.

FAMILY LIFE, JEWISH

The contemporary Jewish family; a review of the social science literature. V.D. Sanua. J Jew Com Ser 50:297-312 Sum '74.

Non-profit family counseling services for the middle class. L. Rohmer. Address. J Jew Com Ser 50:359-66 Sum '74.

New family structures; challenges to family casework. M.W. Levine. Address. J Jew Com Ser 50: 238-44 Sp '74.

The family I. Alternative family forms: communal households and the emerging "post biological family." R.M. Kanter. Rel Ed 69:177-84 Mr/Ap '74.

The family II. An overall view of the family cluster experience: historically, leadership-wise, family-wise. M. Sawin. Rel Ed 69:184-92 Mr/Ap '74.

Drugs and Jewish youth. W.J. Leffler. cond Jew Digest 19:15-18 Ap '74.

Family reunion. L.H. Farber. Commentary 57:38-42 Ja '74.

The problem of loneliness and uselessness. M.L. Brill. Recon 39:23-6 D '73.

Toward enriching the quality of Jewish life: the role of the Jewish family and children's agency. T.R. Isenstadt. Address. J Jew Com Ser 50:31-9 Fall '73.

Toward enriching the quality of Jewish life: after 75 years, a look ahead. R.I. Heller. Address. J Jew Com Ser 50:5-12 Fall '73.

The Jewish family agency: individual and group casework services that build Jewish identity. D. Zeff. Address. J Jew Com Ser 49:303-8 Sum '73M.

The drop-in center: its role in servicing troubled youth. N.R. Keane. Address. J Jew Com Ser 49:225-32 Sp '73.

Strengthening Jewish commitment. C. Zibbell. Address. J Jew Com Ser 49:199-205 Sp '73.

An American family. S. Sanborn. Commentary 55:78-80 My '73.

FEMINISM - see Sex Roles, Women

FERTILITY

Jewish fertility trends and differentials: an examination of the evidence from the census of 1970. R.K. Watts. Jew SS 42:293-312 Sum/Fall '80.

Pinpointing the fertile period for conception and contraception. il M. Kretzmer. Had Mag 62:14-15+ Ag-S '80.

Religiosity and fertility: how strong a connection? Bernard Lazerwitz. Contemporary Jewry 1980, 5, 1, Spring-Summer, 56-63.

News and comments: The Trojan dove; Popularity poll; South-of-the-border oil; Saudi weakness bared; F-15 parts from Israel; Stowaway; Bar Mitzvah at thirty; Soviet propaganda attack; A Solomonic solution; Rabbi on test-tube baby; Clinic for camels. Had Mag 60:35-9 O '78.

Zero population growth. Feminism and Jewish survival. B. Greenberg. il Had Mag 60:12-13+ O '78.

News and comments. D.J. Replogle. Had Mag 56:6-8 F '75.

The biomedical challenges to law and mortality. M.H. Elovitz. Jud 24:144-56 Sp '75.

Birth of a new row between the chief of rabbis. Jew Ob 23:11-12 D 20 '74.

Motivational factors and socio-economic characteristics of vasectomized males. K.L. Kohll. Journal of Biosocial Science 1973, 5, 2, Apr, 169-177.

HANDICAPPED

A voiceless message. N. King. cond Jew Digest 19:33-5 F '74.

To open the ears of the deaf. H. Schwartz. Con Jud 28:59-63 W '74.

Interview: Helping the handicapped; Mm. Rafsel's busy world. R. Portrait. Jew Ob 23:17 f 1 '74.

Special education. Bureau of Jewish Education, Atlanta, Georgia; Bureau of Jewish Education, Cincinnati, Ohio; Congregation Beth Am, Cleveland Heights, Ohio; United Synagogue of America, New York (city). Ped Rep 25:15-16 W '74.

HANDICAPPED

The North Bellmore experience: a proposed community model for Jewish special education. B. and H.E. Greenberg. Syn Sch 31:26-30 Sum '73.

HAVUROT

Speaking of prayer. R. Poretsky. Response 13:143-8 Fall-W '82.

Celebrate havurot! C.A. Sheingold. Moment 7:5 Je '82.

Combining two worlds. M. Rosenberg. Israel Scene 34 F '82.

A study of havurot in five synagogues in the Los Angeles area. H. Wasserman; G.B. Bubis; A. Lert. Jew SS 43:59-74 W '81.

The motherhood of God. D. Levenberg. il Shraga Weil. Nat Jew Mo 95:6-8 Mr '81.

From Somerville to Savannah and Los Angeles and Dayton. W. Novak. Moment 6:17-21+ Ja-F '81.

How to start a havurah. Present Tense 7:30 Sp '80.

Communication: havurah. G. Bubis; R. Libowitz. J Reform Jud 27:76 W '80.

The synagogue, the havurah, and liable communities. L.A. Hoffman. Response No. 38:37-41 '80.

Too many for a minyan. M. Strassfeld. Response No. 38:21-8 '80.

On pseudo-havurology. S. Mowshowitz. Letter. Response No. 38:83-4 '80.

Havurah update. R.G. Monson. Response 12:88 Sum '80.

The reawakening of Jewish religious life in America: Havurot. M Strassfeld. Present Tense 7:29-31 Sp '80.

The concept of havurah: an analysis. H. Wasserman; G.B. Bubis; A. Lert. J Reform Jud 26:35-50 W '79.

The first national havurah conference. J. Oboler. Cong Mo 46:12-13 D '79.

A gathering of communities. E.S. Cohen. Cong Mo 46:13-14 D '79.

HAVUROT

Havurot: progress or pandemonium? A. Gumbiner. cond Jew Digest 25:14-20 N '79.

Communication: havuroth. R. Libowitz. J Reform Jud 26:54 Sum '79.

Communication: havuroth. J. Newsner. J Reform Jud 26:10 Sum '79.

On our minds. "Conflict in the havurot: veterans vs. newcomers." S.M. Cohen. Response 12:3-4+ Sum '79.

Havurot: panacea or pandemonium. A. Gumbiner. Recon 45:19-27 Je '79.

The synagogue havurah -- an experiment in restoring adult fellowship to the Jewish community. D.J. Elazar; R.G. Monson. Jew J Soc 21:67-80 Je '79.

Havurot. Two views. M. Gellman; C. Silberman. Moment 4:62-4 S '79.

The forthcoming havurah conference. Editorial. Recon 44:4-5 F '79.

The impact of the havurah. B. Reisman. cond Jew Digest 23:77-82 Sum '78.

What's a havurah? B. Pash; M. Silver. Present Tense 5:6-8 Sp '78.

The havurah experience. H. Wasserman. J Psychology and Jud 3:168-83 Sp '78.

Professional leadership for the havurah. B. Reisman. CCARJ 24:51-63 W '77.

The havurah as an extended family. A.N. Weiss. Address. J Jew Com Ser 54:135-7 W '77.

The 'establishment' turns to havurot. R. Geberer. cond Jew Digest 22:8-10 Sum '77.

Havura in the ivory tower; a letter from Princeton. H. and E.F. Levine. il Stu Copans. Nat Jew Mo 91:24-7 Je '77.

The havurah experience. (Los Angeles, California) S. King, et al. Recon 43:15-19 My '77.

HAVUROT

Letter. R.A. Siegel. Moment 2:5 Ap '77.

William Novak's article "The future of havurah Judaism." Letter R.A. Siegel. Ap '77.

Alternate Jewish education: the havurah model. il. I. Aron; J. Greenspan; J. Rous; M. Wolf. Response 10:185-92 Sum/Fall '76.

Looking back at the havurah. J. Reimer. Response 10:243-6 Sum/Fall '76.

Historical and contemporary Havurot: a comparison. M. Mayman. J Jew Com Ser 52:361-4 Sum '76.

A rationale and conceptualization for a new rite of passage. S. Stroiman. Recon 42:26-8 Je '76.

A great happening in Boston; revolt of the young. S. Rothchild. Present Tense 3:21-6 Sp '76.

Have you sold out? A Response symposium. Response 10:33-86 Sp '76.

Three havurot. Reprint. A.J. Wolf. Jew Digest 21:25-7 F '76.

The basics of congregational havurot. D. Polish. Recon 41:7-12 D '75.

The havurah: an approach to humanizing Jewish organizational life. B. Reisman. Address. J Jew Com Ser 52:202-9 W '75.

To pursue justice. A. Waskow. Letter. Response No. 24:118-21 W '74/'75.

Transforming Rabbi and congregants. Jewish renewal. S.B. Jacobs. CCARJ 22:37-40 W '75.

Three havurot. Our best hope. A.J. Wolf. CCARJ 22:34-6 W '75.

The evolution of Ezrat Nashim. A. Silverstein. Con Jud 30:41-51 Fall '75.

Not standing - wrestling: sumposium. A.I. Waskow. Reply. Jud 23:464-6 Fall '74.

A call for holy discontent. H. Schulweis. Un Syn Rev 26:8-9 W '74.

HAVUROT

Synagogues are not for always. P.E. Schechter. cond Jew Digest 19:1-4 Je '74.

Let's havurize the synagogue. H. Schulweis. cond Jew Digest 19:1-4 My '74.

Nuclear family loneliness. T. Weiss-Rosmarin. Jew Spec 39:8-10 Sum '74.

On leaving the havurah. W. Novak. Response No. 22:107-15 Sum '74.

A report on the havurot gathering. L. Levin. Response 21:109-17 Sp '74.

Chavurat hamidbar. S. Karni. Letter. Cong bi-W 41:23 N 8 '74.

The Supreme Court and the havurot. J.B. Robison; J. Schatz. Cong bi-W 41:12-13 S 27 '74.

New Jewish consciousness on campus. G.E. Johnson. cond Jew Digest 19:13-17 D '73.

The para-professional in synagogue life: a new approach. A.D. Sorosky. Recon 39:19-23 D '73.

Havurat noar of Los Angeles. D. Engel; J.F. Rothmann. Ped Rep 25:8-10 Fall '73.

HOLOCAUST SURVIVORS

Defending ourselves. A. Donat. Present Tense 9:32-3 W '82.

The world gathering of the Jewish holocaust survivors. Notes of a survivor's son. A. Gerson. Mid 28:28-31 Ap '82.

Special issue on holocaust survivors and survivor's children. Journal of Psychology and Judaism, ed. Rewen P. Bulka. Fall/Winter 1981.

Reflections of a child of holocaust survivors. M.Z. Rosensaft. Mid 27:31-3 N '81.

Differing adaptational styles in families of survivors of the Nazi holocaust. Yael Danieli. Children Today, Vol. 10, No. 5, pp. 6-10, 34-35, Sep-Oct 1981.

HOLOCAUST SURVIVORS

The group project for holocaust survivors and their children. Yael Danieli. Children Today, Vol. 10, No. 5, pp. 11, 33, Sep-Oct 1981.

Adolescents of parent survivors of concentration camps: a review of the literature. E.E. Kuperstein. J Psychology and Jud 6:7-22 Fall/W '81.

A proposal for treating adolescent offspring of holocaust survivors. S. Schneider. J Psychology and Jud 6:68-76 Fall/W '81.

Second generation effects of the holocaust: the effectiveness of group therapy in the resolution of the transmission of parental trauma. F. Kinsler. J Psychology and Jud 6:53-68 Fall/W '81.

Is there a survivor's syndrome? Psychological and socio-political implications. J.N. Porter. J Psychology and Jud 6:33-52 Fall/W '81.

Lessons from world gathering of holocaust survivors. I. Lerner. Jew Ed 49:12-16 Fall '81.

He who saves one life. M. Halperin. il Moment 6:37-41 Jl-Ag '81.

The children of holocaust survivors: isues of separation. C. Katz. J Jew Com Ser 47:257-63 Sp '81.

Do Israeli and diaspora responses to holocaust differ? Symposium S. Efroymson. Reprint. cond Jew Digest 27;20-4 S '81.

Belief and unbelief after the holocaust. R.R. Brenner. Excerpt his The faith and doubt of holocaust survivors. Jew Pec 46:31-5 Sp '81.

We have survived. E. Michel. cond Jew Digest 27:17-19 S '81.

Child of the holocaust. D. Bronsen. Mid 27:50-6 Ap '81.

The holocaust. Woman of valor. S. Cohen. Israel Scene 6-7 Ja '81.

The holocaust and Jewish survival. I. Shorsch. Address. Mid 27:38-42 Ja '81.

Unusual holocaust legacy: survivors and families to meet in Israel. H. Koevary. Israel Scene 8-9 Jl '80.

A legacy of displaced persons -- a personal chronicle. G.D. Schiff. Address. J Jew Com Ser 56:310-5 Sum '80.

HOLOCAUST SURVIVORS

Witness. A. Appelfeld. Jerusalem Q No. 16:91-6 Sum '80.

Surviving and meaning. D. Stone. Jew Spec 44:56-8 W '79.

I survived. Z.S. Kubar. Jew Spec 44:18-20 Fall '79.

Warsaw ghetto boy found alive. J. Finkelstone. cond Jew Digest 24:144-17 My '79.

I remember ... A. Becker. Jew Spec 44:34 Sp '79.

Holocaust survivors, adaptation to trauma. D. Laub. Pat Prej 13:17-25 Ja-F '79.

"The fourth Reich" -- German-Jewish religious life in America today. M.N. Dobkowski. Jud 25:80-95 W '78.

The holocaust was about me. D. Preston. cond Jew Digest 24:59-61 N '78.

Mother of the ghetto. D.C. Gross. cond Jew Digest 24:14-15 O '78.

Where is Yosselle? cond Jew Digest 24:23-4 O '78.

On crucifying the Jews. M. Brown. Jud 27:476-88 Fall '78.

Breaking silence: serving children of holocaust survivors. M. Trachtenberg; M. Davis. J Jew Com Ser 54:294-302 Sum '78.

Studying the holocaust's impact today: some dilemmas of language and method. A. Eckardt. Jud 27:222-32 Sp '78.

A survivor speaks. I. Jerison. cond Jew Digest 24:6-7 S '78.

I liberated Dachau ... W.J. Fellenz. Address. excerpt. Jew Digest 24:3-5 S '78.

The survivor as parent. H. Frankel. J Jew Com Ser 54:241-6 Sp '78.

Jewish GIs and holocaust survivors. A. Grobman. Jew Spec 43:49-52 Sp '78.

The holocaust and the age of absurdity. S. Novins. Recon 44:11-13 My '78.

Children of survivors. M.I. Ludzki. Jew Spec 42:41-3 Fall '77.

HOLOCAUST SURVIVORS

Editors' wrapup. Had Mag 58:9 Je/Jl '77.

Surviving the holocaust. L. Baron. J Psychology and Jud 1:25-37 Sp '77.

The secret hidden in my family portrait. A. Kurzweil. Keeping Posted 23:6-8 S '77.

Bringing home the bride. J. Millman. Moment 2:52-6 Ap '77.

Survival imperatives after the holocaust. R.T. Alpert. Address. Recon 43:7-11 Ap '77.

Social Psychiatry and the Holocaust. Isaac Kanter. Journal of Psychology and Judaism, Vol. 1, No. 1, Fall 1976, pp. 55-66.

Children of the holocaust. Helen Epstein. Present Tense, Vol. 3, No. 4, Summer 1976, pp. 21-25.

Growing up in America with a holocaust heritage. T. Mostysser. Jew Digest 20:3-6 Je '75.

Logotherapy as a response to the holocaust. R.P. Bulka. Trad 15:89-96 Sp-Sum '75.

The vigil. O.R. Yufe. World Over 36:12-13 Mr 28 '75.

Guilt feelings in concentration camp survivors: comments of a survivor. Felicia Carmelly. J Jew Com Ser Winter 1975, vol. Lll, No. 2.

Survival and guilt feelings of Jewish concentration camp victims. G. Schneider. Jew SS 37:74-83 Ja '75.

Meeting the first Jewish survivor. I. Klein. Excerpt his The anguish and ecstasy of a Jewish chaplain. Jew Digest 20:17-21 N '74.

The Selvino children. B. Holtz. cond Jew Digest 20:56-9 O '74.

The survivor. M. Millstone. Jew Spec 39:54 Sum '74.

Survival and witness. L.C. Dubin. Jew Fron 41:23-5 Ap '74.

HOMOSEXUALITY

A Jewish minority speaks up for its rights. J. Rosenfeld. cond <u>Jew</u> <u>Digest</u> 27:12-15 N '81.

Another religious view of gay leberation. J.B. Miller. cond <u>Jew</u> <u>Digest</u> 24:40-4 Jl/Ag '79.

Homosexuality: clinical and ethical challenges. M.H. Spero. <u>Trad</u> 19;53-73 Sp '79.

The closet: another religious view of gay liberation. J.B. Miller. <u>Reconstructionist,</u> Vol. 44, Fall 1979, pp. 18-25.

Attitudes toward premarital, extramarital, and homosexual relations in the U.S. in the 1970s. Norval D. Glenn; Charles N. Weaver. <u>Journal</u> <u>of</u> <u>Sex</u> <u>Research</u> 1979, 15,2, May, 108-118.

Are homosexuals gay? S. McCracken. <u>Commentary</u> 67:19-29 Ja '79.

Sin, crime, sickness or alternative lifestyle? A Jewish approach to homosexuality. H.J. Matt. <u>Jud</u> 27:13-24 W '78.

Homosexuality: a Jewish perspective. B.D. Schwartz. <u>Un</u> <u>Syn</u> <u>Rev</u> 30:4-5+ Sum '77.

Homosexuality and the Jewish tradition. A. Bar-Zev. <u>Recon</u> 42:20-4 My '76.

Letter to the editor: disappointed with responsum. A. Green. <u>CCARJ</u> 21:78-9 W '74.

Who is the liberal? S.B. Freehof. Letter. <u>CCARJ</u> 21:79-80 W '74.

Not a Jewish lifestyle option. Letter. G. Kollin. <u>CCARJ</u> 20:94-5 Sum '74.

Auden's achievement. C. James. <u>Commentary</u> 56:53-8 D '73.

Homosexuality and Jewish tradition. S.B. Freefoh. cond <u>Jew</u> <u>Digest</u> 18;30-2 Ag '73.

Gay reform. S. Spiegler. <u>J</u> <u>Jew</u> <u>Com</u> <u>Ser</u> 49:329-30 Sum '73.

Homosexuals and the Jews. E. Raab. cond <u>Jew</u> <u>Digest</u> 18:25-6 Ap '73.

A question of identity. A. Lasker. <u>Forum</u> No. 44:59-67 Sp '82.

IDENTITY, JEWISH

Working her way back. F.B. Maynard. Present Tense 9:12-15 Sp '82.

Roots: 'lost generation' return. C. Novis. Israel Scene 15-16 Mr '82.

Orthodox cooperation with non-Orthodoxy. W.S. Wurzburger. Jew Life 5:25-7 Sum/Fall '81.

Will our children remain Jewish in America? L.C. Pogrebin. Cong Mo 48;12-14 My '81.

Breaking the faith. Commentary and the American Jews. B. Avishai. Moment 6:67-74 Mr/Ap '81.

Who is a Jew? W. Kramer. Letter. Moment 6:9 N '81.

Jewish connectionss. L. Fein. Moment 6:15-19 N '81.

Renewable identity. D.J. Elazar. Mid 27:28-30 Ja '81.

Interpersonal, nonverbal, and small group communication: abstracts of doctoral dissertations published in Dissertation Abstracts International, July through December 1981 (Vol. 42, Nos. 1 through 6). ERIC Clearinghouse on Reading and Communication Skills, Urbana, Ill. 1988, 19p.

Teaching about the role of women. G. Rosen. Ped Rep 32:27-30 Fall '80.

The Jewish response to crisis. M. Ostrow. Con Jud 33:3-25 Sum '80.

The study of American Jewish identification: how it is defined, measured, obtained, sustained and lost. Harold S. Himmelfarb. Journal for the Scientific Study of Religion 1980, 19, 1, Mar, 48-60.

A matter of choice: Jewish identity in the coming generation. A. Hareven. Address. J Jew Com Ser 56:215-26 Sp '80.

The dynamics of Jewish identity. L. Smolar. J Jew Com Ser 56:278-81 Sp '80.

Of Jewish roots. Essay. D. Bar-Nathan. Shefa 3:69-76 '80.

For a personal crisis of identity among the young. A. Hertzberg. Symposium. Jew Fron 47:10-11 D '79.

Why Jewishness? H.I. Bogot. J Jew Com Ser 56:106-7 Fall '79.

IDENTITY, JEWISH

The trouble with Reform Judaism. J. Weinberg. Commentary 68:53-60 N '79.

The quest for Jewish identity in a changing social milieu. A. Lor. Rel Ed 74:173-80 Mr-Ap '79.

Patterns of contemporary Jewish identity. S.N. Eisenstadt. Ariel No. 48:4-16 '79.

The new ethnicity, religious survival and Jewish identity: the Judaisms of our newest members. David Ellenson. Journal of Reform Judaism, Spring 1979, pp. 47-60.

Education for Jewish identity and Jewish continuity in the open society. Z. Slesinger. Jud 28:225-35 Sp '79.

American Jewry today: ethnicity and assimilation. J. Neusner. cond Jew Digest 23:3-9 Sum '78.

An approach to the components and consequences of Jewish identification. Bernard Lazerwitz. Contemporary Jewry 1978, 4, 2, Spring-Summer, 3-8.

Erik Erikson's Jewishness. M.H. Spero. Mid 23:76-82 Je/Jl '77.

Becoming Jewish. H. Polt. Mid 23:64-6 Mr '77.

Strengthening Jewish identity in a residential setting. Simcha Goldman. J Jew Com Ser, Vol. LIII, No. 2, Winter 1976, pp. 165-170.

The Jewish professional and Jewish identity. R.P. Zager. Address. J Jew Com Ser 53:141-6 W '76.

Creating Jewish identity in Ames, Iowa. Harold I. Sharlin. Sh'ma, Vol. 7, No. 122, November 26, 1976, pp. 10-12.

The crisis of identity in the dynamics of Jewish life. E. Rivkin. Symposium. Jew Ed 45:4-16+ Fall-W '76.

Who is a Jewish child? Solomon D. Goldfarb. Conservative Judaism, Vol. XXX, No. 4, Summer 1976, pp. 309.

Jewish identity: its use for clinical purposes. F. Berl. J Jew Com Ser 52:344-54 Sum '76.

IDENTITY, JEWISH

Our people; Friday afternoon Jew. T.J. Cottle. Moment 1:45-8 Ja '76.

Translating Jewish commitment into practice. L. Fein. Address. J Jew Com Ser 52:10-16 Fall '75.

Why I am a Jew. Excerpts. Jew Life 51-8 Tishrei 5736 (Fall '75).

Rediscovering the soul in Jewish communal practice. S. Hofstein. Address. Comment on L. Fein's article, Translating Jewish commitment into practice. J Jew Com Ser 52:17-19 Fall '75.

Therefore choose life. J.R. Levenson. Commentary 60:52-6 N '75.

The quest for Jewishness: American Jews' I.D. dilemma. R. Kestenbaum. Israel 6:46-50 No. 11 '74/'75.

Teaching and commemorating the holocaust: as a vehicle to strengthen Jewish identity. E. Frankel. Ped Rep 25:H-11-12 W '74.

Prejudice in young children. A.G. Davey. Pat Prej 8:17-22 My/Je '74.

On American Jewish identity. C.I. Waxman. Cong bi-W 41:17-19 S 27 '74.

On teaching Jewish identity. E. Wiesel. Address. Jew Ed 43:8-13 W/Sp '75.

Some notes for survival. F. Perlmutter. J Jew Com Ser 50;195-7 W '73.

Games that explore Jewish identity. P. Feuerstein. cond Jew Digest 19:35-8 O '73.

Returning us to ourselves. L. Edelman. Editorial. Jew Heritage 15:3-6 Sum/Fall '73.

Restructuring the synagogue. H.M. Schulweis. Con Jud 27;13-24 Sum '73.

INTELLIGENCE

In defense of intelligence tests. R.J. Herrnstein. Commentary 69:40-51 F '80.

INTELLIGENCE

The interaction concept and the gifted child. H. Abramowitz. Ped Rep 31:35-6 Fall '79.

Education of the gifted and talented: some basic principles. A.H. Passow. Excerpt his The gifted and the talented: their education and development. Ped Rep 31:5-7 Fall '79.

Problems of equality. William Silverman. Jew Spec 41:75 sum '76.

Patterns of intellectual ability in Jewish and Arab children in Israel: II. Urban matched samples. Amia Lieblich; and others. Journal of Cross-Cultural Psychology, 6, 2, 218-226, Jun 1975.

INTERGENERATIONAL - see Parent-Child Relationship

INTERMARRIAGE - see Mixed Marriage

JEWISH COMMUNAL LIFE - see Community Life, Jewish

MARRIAGE

Meshedi marriage traditions. I.G. Cowen. cond Jew Digest 27:22-6 F '82.

Reading the Jewish tradition on marital sexuality. E.B. Borowitz. J Reform Jud 29:1-15 Sum '82.

Lasting marriage: Jewish style. B. Schlesinger; R.B. Mullaly. J Jew Com Ser 59:249-52 Sp '82.

We're having too much fun, oy, to marry. D. Dorfman. cond Jew Digest 27:75-80 Ap '82.

Sex and the single God. H.M. Schulweis. Recon 47:17-26 N '81.

Is there still room for the Rebbetzin today? S.D. Schwartzman. J Reform Jud 28:64-6 fall '81.

Orthodoxy responds to feminist ferment. S. Berman; S. Magnus. Response 12:5-17 Sp '81.

Guest comments: a rabbi writes to his congregants. J.D. Bleich. Jew Life 4:8-10 Fall '80.

Race, equality and the law. D. Pearl. Pat Prej 14:3-9 O '80.

MARRIAGE

Sex in Judaism. R. Gordis. Excerpt his Love and sex: a modern Jewish perspective. Jew Spec 45:17-21 Sum '80.

Matchmaking and love. M. Lamm. Excerpt his The Jewish way in love and marriage. Jew Spec 45:22-8 Sum '80.

Something old, something new. C. Yalkut. il Nat Jew Mo 94:4-9 Ja '80.

Chronicle. Jew J Soc 21:181-6 D '79.

Midrash. A.E. Kitov. Moment 4:26-7 Je '79.

Seven bindings. R. Ben-David. Moment 4:28-32 Je '79.

A walnut tree, a glass of wine, and thou. P.R. Eisenberg. Moment 4:34-8 Je '79.

A San Joaquin valley marriage -- 1894. West States Jew Hist Q 11:113 Ja '79.

Perspective. Zenter-Marriage. W. Blank. Moment 4:4-10 D '78.

The women's role. C.H. Pearl. Con Jud 32:67-70 Fall '78.

Meditations on a marriage ı do, I do? il T. Cottle. Moment 3:24-8 Je '78.

I do, I do? pt 2. T. Cottle. il Moment 3:50-7 Jl/Ag '78.

Anglo-Jewry: Marriage statistics inconclusive. N. Grizzard. Jew Ob 26:18 Ag 4 '77.

A ceremonial crux: removing a man's sandal as a female gesture of contempt. C.M. Carmichael. J Bib Lit 96:321-36 S '77.

Annulment of marriage within the context of the Get. A. Rakeffet-Rothkoff. Trad 15:173-85 Sp-Sum '75.

Courtship and arranged marriages among Eastern European Jews prior to World War I as· depicted in a Briefenshteller. Nathan Hurvitz. Journal of Marriage and the Family 1975, 37, 2, May, 422-430.

The sacred marriage rite. S.N. Kramer. il Ariel No. 37:62-86 '74.

MARRIAGE

The pregnant bride; a responsum. S.B. Freehof. CCARJ 21:24-6 W '74.

In defense of monogamy. G. Gilder. Commentary 58:31-6 N '74.

Is marriage obsolete? A.S. Maller. Recon 40:7-10 F '74.

Is marriage a private affair? H.E. Schaalman. Keeping Posted 19:22-3 F '74.

Love and marriage: some questions for Jews. C.A. Kroloff. Keeping Posted 19:L3-7 F '74.

Some romantic Jewish marriage customs. D. Davidovitch. cond Jew Digest 18:38-44 Jl '73.

Marriage and household. S. Rudikoff. Commentary 54:56-64 Je '73.

How to catch a man. T. Avidar. Israel 5:12+ Sp '73.

Marriage, old style. M.S. Shapiro. Jew Digest 18:81 Ja '73.

MENTAL RETARDATION - see Special Education, Children

MIXED MARRIAGE

Report on committee on patrilineal descent of children of mixed marriages. CCAR, April 1983.

Are we ready for the new Jewish community? J.A. Edelheit. J Reform Jud 29:14-20 W '82.

From Christianity to Judaism: religion changers in American society. S. Huberman. Con Jud 36:10-18 Fall '82.

Coping with intermarriage. J.D. Sarna. Jew Spec 47:26-8 Sum; cond Jew Digest 28:12-15 N '82.

"Keruv" and the status of intermarried families. J. Roth; D. Gordis. Con Jud 35:50-5 Sum '82.

The mitzvah of keruv. J.B. Agus. Con Jud 35:33-8 Sum '82.

The status of a non-Jewish spouse and children of a mixed-marriage in the synagogue. K. Abelson. Con Jud 35:39-49 Sum '82.

MIXED MARRIAGE

Interreligious marriages in the United States: patterns and recent trends. Norval D. Glenn. Journal of Marriage and the Family 1982, 44, 3, Aug, 555-566.

Accounting for Jewish intermarriage: an assessment of national and community studies. Bernard Farber; Leonard Gordon. Contemporary Jewry 1982, 6, 1, Spring-Summer, 47-75.

Rifts in the Jewish community. J.J. Petuchowski. Jew Spec 47:17-19 Sp '82.

The end. R. Greengard. Letter. Present Tense 9:4 Sp '82.

Jewish intermarriage. S. Rosen. Mid 28;30-4 Mr '82.

Reflections on assimilation in America. J. Braun. Mid 28:24-6 F '82.

Jewish-Christian marriages and conversions. B. Lazerwitz. Jew SS 43:31-46 W '81.

A preparation for marriage to a Jew. Leslie Simon. Journal of Reform Judaism, Summer 1981.

A clinician's view of intermarriage. Herberg Strean. J Jew Com Ser, Summer 1981.

Communication: A. Goldstein. J Reform Jud 28:100-1 Sp '81.

Intermarriage in Britain and the United States. R.T. Schaefer. Pat Prej 15:8-15 Ap '81.

Mixed marriages and race realtions today. C. Bagley. Pat Prej 15:33-44 ja '81.

A light unto the nations. N. Datan. Moment 6:49-51 D '80.

Letter: N. Mirsky on mixed dating, etc. H. Engelsohn. Moment 6:4 D '80.

The shiksa question. Moment 5:22-5 Jl-Ag '80.

Intermarriage. A.S. Axelrad. Excerpt The third Jewish catalog. eds. S. and M. Strassfeld. Present Tense 7:53 Sum '80.

A modern midrash on Psalm one. A.S. Maller. J Reform Jud 24:85-6 Sum '80.

MIXED MARRIAGE

Children of mixed marriages. Reconstructionist, March 1980.

Black humiliation and Jewish martyrdom. A.A. Mazrui. Pat Prej 13:1-7 S '79.

Half-Jew; sooner or later the children grow up. P. Span. Present Tense 6:49-52 Sum '79.

On intermarriage and Jewish education. A.I. Schiff. Jew Ed 47:18-21 Sum '79.

Living with intermarriage. D. Singer. Commentary 68:48-53 Jl '79.

A cure for intermarriage? E. Mayer. Moment 4:62+ Je '79.

Vital signs. L. Fein. Moment 4:11-14 Je '79.

To the editor. E. Mayer. J Jew Com Ser 55:299-301 Sp '79.

Jews and non-Jews: falling in love. S. Huberman. Address. J Jew Com Ser 55:265-79 Sp '79.

Alternating moods. Editorial. Recon 45:4-5 Sp '79.

Intermarriage and Jewish identity: the implications for pluralism and assimilation in American society. Bernard Farber; Leonard Gordon; Albert J. Mayer. Ethnic and Racial Studies 1979, 2, 2, Apr, 222-230.

Reaching in, reaching out. Dealing with the Jewish population problem. A. Schindler. Moment 4:20-3 Mr '79.

Comments; "Stop the press"; Where are we at? Israel's new government; Orthodoxy: an alternative lifestyle. Y. Jacobs. Jew Life 2:2-6 Fall/W '77-78.

To the editor. A.S. Maller. J Jew Com Ser 55:122-4 Autumn '78.

The intermarriage ripoff. D. Schwartz. Moment 3:62-4 Jl/Ag '78.

Rethinking the inter-marriage crisis. F. Massarik. Moment 3:29-33 Je '78.

A comparison of intergenerational relations in the Jewish and non-Jewish family. Gerald Cromer. Adolescence, 13, 50, 297-309, Sum '78.

MIXED MARRIAGE

Must intermarriage lead to doomsday? F. Massarik. cond Jew Digest 24:8-13 O '78.

On "Mitzva marriages." J.S. Rubenfeld. Amer Zion 69:37 S/O '78.

Queen Esther and intermarriage today. A.S. Maller. cond Jew Digest 23:39-41 Mr '78.

Responsa. E.J. Lipman. Nat Jew Mo 92:11 Ja '78.

Intermarried couples who cope. It's a cinch if you reduce your commitment. M. Silver. Nat Jew Mo 92:10-16 Ja '78.

For mitzva marriages. A.S. Maller. Amer Zion 68:36-7 Ja '78.

Responsa. O. Groner. Nat Jew Mo 92:11 Ja '78.

American Jewish college youth. Changing identity. C.I. Waxman. Forum No. 2:35-44 '77.

Contra mixed marriages: some historical and theological reflections. B. Martin. Symposium. CCARJ 24:75-85 Sum '77.

Coping with intermarriage. G. Rosenblatt. cond Jew Digest 23:9-12 S '77.

Intermarriage and Jewish continuity. A.S. Maller. cond Jew Digest 22:56-82 My '77.

We are many; our readers speak on intermarriage. Moment 2:34-8 Ap '77.

On mixed marriages. H. Cohn. Letter. Recon 43:27-8 Mr '77.

Reader opinion poll (on intermarriage). Moment 2:63-4 Ja '77.

Intermarriage and Jewish continuity. A.S. Maller. Cong Mo 43:14-15 O '76.

Rabbinic ethics and mixed marriage: an exercise in "Catch 22." N. Kominsky. CCARJ 23:64-6 Autumn '76.

Communication (Mixed marriage). E. Yoffie. CCARJ 23:90 Sum '76.

Mixed marriage and Reform rabbis. A.S. Maller. Jud 24:39-48 W '75.

MIXED MARRIAGE

Arabs and Jews. R. Gordis. Letter. Reply T. Weiss-Rosmarin.
Jew Spec 40:72-3 W '75.

Jewish-gentile divorce in California. Allen S. Maller. Jewish Social
Studies 1975, 37, 3-4, Sum-Fall, 279-290.

Intermarriage we shall overcome. S. Spiegler. J Jew Com Ser
52:105 Fall '75.

Religious education and interfaith marriage. A.S. Maller. Ped Rep
27:29-32+ Fall '75.

Mixed (up) marriage. S. Rosenkranz. co nd Jew Digest 20:69-70 F
'75.

Jewish-gentile intermarriage: definitions and consequences. James S.
Frideres; Jay E. Godlstein. Social Compass 1974, 21, 1, 69-84.

American Jews and exogamy. Two sets of influences. A.S. Maller.
CCARJ 21:63-7 Autumn '74.

Intermarriage and communal survival in a London suburb. G. Cromer.
Jew J Soc 16:155-69 D '74.

Napoleon's third question. A.A. Chiel. Jew Digest 20:70-2 D '74.

Jewry's future. E. Mayer. Letter. Reply H. Goldmeier. Cong bi-W
41:2+ N 8 '74.

The new dissident group in Reform Judaism. Editorial. Recon 40:4-6
N '74.

Yet more thoughts on intermarriage. G. Kollin. Recon 40:18-23 O
'74.

From my alienated vantage; symposium. Reply. H.L. Feingold. Jud
23:408-11 Fall '74.

Towards the development of a planned communal response to Jewish
intermarriage. J. Hochbaum. J Jew Com Ser 51:131-8 W '74.

The new Reform and authority. D. Polish. Jud 23:8-22 W '74.

"Guess who's coming to dinner?" Intermarriage in three countries.
B. Buckley. Present Tense 1:13-14 W '74.

MIXED MARRIAGE

The roots of intermarriage. C.U. Lipshitz. Jew Life 41:30-6 Sum '74.

Chronicle. Jew J Soc 16:109-16 Je '74.

Converting because of marriage motives. M.S. Goodblatt. Con Jud 28:30-40 Sp '74.

Small town Jewry. J Jew Com Ser 50:272-3 Sp '74.

Love and gentiles -- righteous or otherwise. S. Dworkin. Nat Jew Mo 88:20-2+ My '74.

Intermarriage, the myth and reality. I. and B. Greenberg. Had Mag 55:32-5 F '74.

From the president. Enough! D. Polish. CCARJ 20:35-7 W '73.

Some dimensions of interreligious marriages in Indiana, 1962-67. Thomas P. Monahan. Social Forces 1973, 52, 2, Dec, 195-203.

Mixed marriage, again. M.S. Shapiro. Jew Digest 19:81 D '73.

The intermarriage issue; crisis and challenge. R. Pelcovitz. Jew Life 41:38-47 O '73.

Sociology of inter-marriage. Gerald B. Bubis. J Jew Com Ser, Fall 1973, Vol. L, No. 1.

Intermarriage, the rabbi, and the Jewish communal worker. G.B. Bubis. J Jew Com Ser 50:85-97 Fall '73.

Mixed marriages pledge by Goren. Jew Ob 22:15 Ag 10 '73.

Parents can block intermarriage. S.S. Fader. Nat Jew Mo 87:28-9 Jl/Ag '73.

Rabbis and mixed marriage. W. Kaelter. Jew Spec 38:11-13 Je '73.

Did Ezra ban all intermarriages? D.M. Eichhorn. CCARJ 20:42-4 Sp '73.

Intermarriage; catastrophe or challenge. W. Abrams. Un Syn Rev 26:12-13+ Sp '73.

MIXED MARRIAGE

Mixed marriage. 1972 convention statment. pt 1 A complex phenomenon. M.I. Rothman. CCARJ 20:L14-17 Sp '73.

Mixed marriage. 1972 convention statement. pt 2 Not to hurt but to heal. H.E. Schaalman. CCARJ 20:17-20 Sp '73.

Mixed marriage. 1972 convention statement. pt 3 Eight questions of halachah. M.B. Ryback. CCARJ 20:21-4 Sp '73.

Mixed marriage. 1972 convention statement. pt 4 The role of the rabbi. N. Kominsky. CCARJ 20:24-8 Sp '73.

Mixed marriage. 1972 convention statement. pt 5 We need a new halachah. P. Gorin. CCARJ 20:28-30 Sp '73.

Mixed marriage. 1972 convention statement. pt 6 Marrying "in" not "out." I.H. Fishbein. CCARJ 20:31-4 Sp '73.

Mixed marriage. 1972 convention statement. pt 7 Realities versus expectations. J.R. Narot. CCARJ 20:34-6 Sp '73.

Mixed marriage. 1972 convention statement. pt 8 Conflict between religion and state. "Sometimes we must say no." L. Baeck. tr J.J. Petuchowski. CCARJ 20:37-41 Sp '73.

Mixed marriage. 1972 convention statement. pt 9 "Judaism and racism incompatible." D.M. Eichhorn. CCARJ 20:42-4 Sp '73.

Mixed marriage. 1972 convention statement. pt 10 The rock of reality. A parable. W.G. Braude. CCARJ 20:44-6 Sp '73.

Mixed marriage. 1972 convention statement. pt 11 Rabbinic referrals. Will the couple be left on their own? R.R. Brenner. CCARJ 20:46-50 Sp '73.

Mixed marriage. 1972 convention statement. pt 12 The ger toshav. An old concept renewed. A.D. Fisher. CCARJ 20:50-4 Sp '73.

Her name shall be Ruth. M.J. Routtenberg. Had Mag 54:22-4 My '73.

Ger toshav and mixed marriage. A.D. Fisher. Recon 39:22-6 My '73.

Offspring of Jewish inter-marriage: a note. James S. Frideres. Jewish Social Studies 1973, 35, 2, Apr, 149-156.

MIXED MARRIAGE

Esther comes home. cond Jew Digest 18:61-2 Mr '73.

Rabbis attack mixed marriage -- and each other. Recon 39:5-6 Mr '73.

The attitude of the non-religious Sabra to Jewish tradition. N. Weinberg. Recon 39:17-24 F '73.

What has happened to the converts? I. Borvick. Jew Life 40:11-16 Ja '73.

PARENT-CHILD RELATIONSHIP

Jewish person to person. Ped Rep 33:15 My '82.

The invisible Jew. Reprint. Keeping Posted 27:8-9 Ap '82.

The way I remember my mother. S.N. Guiora. cond Jew Digest 27:38-40 Ja '82.

My father, Mordecai. J.K. Eisenstein. Jud 30:11-14 W '81.

Learning together: a program for parents and children. M. Feinberg. Pedagic Forum in Ped Rep 32:31-2 W '81.

Children's responsibility to parents. Keeping Posted 37:15 O '81.

Parent's responsibility to children. Keeping Posted 37:14 O '81.

The sandwich generation: adult children of the aging. Dorothy Miller. Social Work, September 1981.

Rav Yitzhak Hutner's lecture to a teachers' conference. tr (from yiddish) S. Carmy. Trad 19:220-6 Fall '81.

Dynamics of the Soviet Jewish family: its impact on clinical practice for the Jewish family agency. P. Hulewat. Address. J Jew Com Ser 58:53-60 Fall '81.

Communications. B.P. King. J Reform Jud 28;80-1 Sum '81.

Family education: Jewish family education program for soviet immigrants; Fathering: changes and challenge; Family education association; Gesher la-bayit. Ped Rep 32:6-8 Ap 81.

Love after death. H.R. Nadich. Jew Spec 45:23-4 W '80.

PARENT-CHILD RELATIONSHIP

Akeda: right brain vs. left. E.W. Sucov. Recon 46:23-5 O '80.

The Akeidah. P.A. Martin. Con Jud 33:41-55 Sum '80.

Sons against their fathers. M.I. Oppenheim. Jud 29:340-52 Sum '80.

A parent's problem. F. Wile. Idea Forum in Ped Rep 31:34 Sp '80.

"Daddy and me" at Sinai temple. B. Salvay. Ped Rep 31:23-4 Sp '80.

Modern problems of Jewish parents. J. Kohn. Excerpts. Recon 45:18-21 Ja '80.

The family in transition; a search for new answers. E. Lauter. Recon 45:13-17 Ja '80.

Parents and children: the first years of life, with bibliography. L. Barber. Review essay. Rel Ed 75:97-100 Ja-F '80.

Between parents and children: the wisdom of Jacob Kohn. Jacob Kohn. Reconstructionist, vol. XLV, #9, January 1980, pp. 17-21.

The Jewish Nursery school as surrogate parent. Marvell Ginsburg. Metropolitan Chicago Board of Jewish Education, Ill. 1980, 14p.

Fathers and sons. L. Kriegel. Present Tense 7:71 Autumn '79.

The parent and special education. R. Layman. Ped Rep 31:21-2 Fall '79.

The editor's corner: to Isaac Toubin; helping the parent; laissez-faire parenthood. Ped Rep 30:1 Fall '78.

A comparison of intergenerational relations in the Jewish and non-Jewish family. Gerald Cromer. Adolescence 1978, 13, 50, Summer, 297-309.

The value of children to parents in the United States. Lois Wladis Hoffman; Arland Thorton; Jean Denby Manis. Journal of Population 1978, 1, 2, Summer, 91-131.

Parental involvement: how the parent should relate to the adolescent's informal Jewish activities. E. Arzt. Ped Rep 29;8-10 Sp '78.

PARENT-CHILD RELATIONSHIP

Breaking the 'Jewish mother' stereotype. R. Oliver. cond Jew Digest 23:13-18 Ja '78.

Trends in Jewish child care. J.L. Taylor. Address. cond J Jew Com Ser 53:93-102 Fall '76.

Your child in foster care. The Jewish Child Care Association of New York. Child Welfare, 55, 2, 125-131, Feb 1976.

Samuel Jacobs and his son, Samuel, Jr. problem child -- 1780-1785. Amer Jew Arc 27:176-83 N '75.

The Jewish father for a change. L. Fuchs. Moment 1:45-50 S '75.

Were women created unequal? M.H. Spero. Jew Life 41:17-21 W '74.

Use of parents' groups in a residential treatment center. L. Siegel. Address. J Jew Com Ser 50:367-71 Sum '74.

A research note on the generation gap in the Orthodox Jewish community. E. Mayer. J Jew Com Ser 50:274-5 Sp '74.

"Now it's our children"; an Israeli mother calls the Yom Kippur War the most terrible war of all. A. Forster. Excerpt. ADL Bull 31:5-6 Mr '74.

Oedipus, Shmeedipus. G. Green. cond Jew Digest 19:49-51 D '73.

Youth-adult confrontation: a symposium. M.F. Baer. Responses M.J. and J. Rosenberg. Recon 39:7-17 F '73.

POPULATION STATISTICS - see Demography

POVERTY see Community Life, Jewish

SEXUALITY

Special issue Keeping Posted 27: Mr 82.

Treating marital and sexual problems in the Orthodox Jewish community. Norman Fertel and Esther Feuer. Journal of Psychology and Judaism, Spring/Summer 1981.

Sexuality and Judaism. J.N. Porter. Recon 44:11-17 F '79.

SEXUALITY

Kol ishah. Lilith No 5:5-9+ d '78.

Some preliminary considerations regarding sex education, counseling and sex therapy and the Jewish tradition. L.S. Kravitz; S. Salkowitz; R.K. Westheimer. J Jew Com Ser 54:282-4 Sum '78.

Sex among teenagers. A.S. Maller. Recon 44:16-21 F '78.

Sex in Judaism. R. Gordis. Excerpt his Love and sex; a modern Jewish perspective. Cong Mo 45:10-13 Ja '78.

Sex change a Talmudic no-no. J.D. Bleich. J Jew Com Ser 54:176 W '77.

Sexuality and religious education. R.P. Craig; C. Middleton, Jr. Rel Ed 72:595-605 N-D '77.

Redefining the goals of sex education. N.S. Goldman. Jew Ed 45:24-32 Sum-Fall '77.

The kedusha of monogamy: a personal perspective. Y. Tsuriel. Response 10:65-70 W '76/'77.

The liberal Jew and sex. E.M. Umansky. Response 10:71-4 W '76/'77.

Sex: professionals and lay people. Neil Shister. Moment, Vol. 2, No. 3, December 1976, pp. 21-23 and 40-42.

Problems rabbis don't talk about. Letter. M.L. Brill. Jew Spec 41:70+ Fall '76.

Is it bed for the Jews? M. Halberstam. Moment 1:28-32 Ap '76.

What Jewish values tell us about sex. W.S. Wurzburger. cond Jew Digest 19:27-30 Mr '74.

Men, women and the parental imperative. D. Gutmann. Commentary 56:59-64 D '73.

Sexism in the Jewish student community. Address. V.S. Salowitz. Response 18:54-8 Sum '73.

Love and eros. E. Livneh. Israel 5:81-4 My '73.

SEXUALITY

Sex and the Jewish college girl. J. Segal. Sermon. cond Jew Digest 18:36-40 Ap '73.

SEX ROLES

Communication. Mrs. N. Share. J Reform Jud 29:57-8 W '82.

Communication. C.L. Felix. J Reform Jud 29:55-7 W '82.

Women and Judaism: a view from tradition. B. Greenberg. Excerpt. Lilith No. 9:5-8 Sp/Sum '82.

Feminism and thought control. M. Levin. Commentary 73:40-4 Je '82.

Not for women only. B. Lamm. Letter. Jew Spec 47:61+ Sp '82.

In Brief. Editorial. Recon 43:6 My '82.

The religious journey of women: the educational task. G. Durka. Rel Ed 77:163-78 Mr-Ap '82.

The status of women in early Israel. C. Meyers. cond Jew Digest 27:30-4 Ja '82.

Between feminism and tradition. B. Morris. il Had Mag 62:16-17+ Je-Jl '81.

Blaming Jews for inventing patriarchy. J. Plaskow. Lilith No. 7:11-12 '80.

The feminish mystique. M. Levin. Commentary 70:25-30 D '80.

Leaders feel powerless. M. Spiegel; R. Lowenthal. Lilith No. 7:41-2 D '80.

Teaching about the role of women. G. Rosen. Ped Rep 32:27-30 Fall '80.

Who has not created me a woman. J.D. Goldberg. Jew Spec 45:29-30 Sum '80.

Sex in Judaism. R. Gordis. Excerpt his Love and sex: a modern Jewish perspective. Jew Spec 45:17-21 Sum '80.

Golda and feminism. P. Lahav. cond Jew Digest 25:23-8 Ap '80.

SEX ROLES

Special issue Keeping Posted 25: F '80.

Orthodox feminists. S. Levine. Photographs Steven Schnur. Keeping Posted 25:19 Ja '80.

Hadassah: choosing powerlessness. T. Kaufman. Lilith No. 6:43 '79.

Notes toward finding the right question. C. Ozick. Forum No. 35:37-60 Sp/Sum '79; Lilith No. 6:19-20 '79.

Women and Jewish education. S.W. Schneider. Reprint. Jew Digest 25:19-27 D '79.

Women in the synagogue: a congregant's view. R.R. Seldin. Con Jud 32:80-8 S '79.

Open forum: a philosophy of Jewish masculinity; one interpretation. R.M. Yellin. Con Jud 32:89-94 W '79.

Women in Jewish life and law. D. Aronson. Jew Spec 44:33-8 Sum '79.

Sexist interpretations. T. Weiss-Rosmarin. Editorial. Jew Spec 44:10+ Sp '79.

World of our mothers. S. Jacoby. Excerpt her The possible she. Present Tense 6:48-51 Sp '79.

Mehizah, Midrash and modernity: a study in religious rhetoric. A.J. Yuter. Jud 28:147-59 Sp '79.

Equality for Jewish women. Letter. R. Gordis. Reply T. Weiss-Rosmarin. Jew Spec 44:57 Sp '79.

Woman's role -- some ultimate concerns. R.P. Bulka. Trad 17:27-40 Sp '79.

A woman at the Torah. S. and A.E. Gould. Recon 45:26-9 My '79.

Letters. D. Toubin; B. Greenberg. Had Mag 60:39-40 D '78.

Women in Jewish schools. G. Lang; M. Carroll; L. Liebman. Jew Ed 47:30-6+ Fall '78.

The portrayal of girls and women in Jewish textbooks and curricula. G. Rosen. Ped Rep 29:20-2 Sp '78.

SEX ROLES

Kol ishah. Lilith 1:7-11 F/W '77/'78.

Esther Broner. S. Windstone, Interview with E. Broner. cond Lilith 1:32-6 F/W '77/'78.

The Jewish establishment is not an equal opportunity employer. A. Stone. Lilith 1:25-6 F/W '77/'78.

Jewish values: Male and female in religion; Gemilut hesed - learning and doing; After-life theories. Ped Rep 28:21-2 W '77.

The Jew as a woman. R. Siegel. Adapt. Jew Spec 42:40-2 W '77.

Commentary and debate: sex and the tradition: a rejoinder. J. Chipman. Response 11:103-6 Fall '77.

Commentary and debate: American feminism and alien philosophy. A.D. Goldman. Response 11:106-8 Fall '77.

Sexual stereotypes. J.P. Isk. Commentary 64:58-64 O '77.

"In a coma! I thought she was Jewish!" S.W. Schneider. Lilith 1:5-8 Sp/Sum '77.

Kol ishah. R. Siegel; S. Seidman; B. Tanenhaus; et al. Lilith 1:22-5 Sp/Sum '77.

Toward a reconstruction of the Jewish family. I.C. Salavan. Letter. Recon 43:29-30 Mr '77.

Letter (sex role). D.E. Kerman. Moment 2:7 F-Mr '77.

Ten women tell ... The ways we are. R. Adler; A.Lee; G. Averbuch; E. Hutt v'Dodd; B. Bauman; E. Sirlin; A. Cohn; J. Rogul; M. Gordon; D. Nagle. Lilith 1:4-14 W '76/'77.

An exclusive interview with Phyllis Chesler. A.C. Suckoff. Lilith 1:24-31 W '76/'77.

The locked cabinet. A. Stone. Lilith 1:17-21 W '76/'77.

Sex: professionals and lay people. N. Shister. Moment 2:21-3+ D '76.

Passivity, equality and the Jewish women. E. Gertel. Cong Mo 43:13-15 N '76.

SEX ROLES

American Jewish men: fear of feminism. B. Lamm. Lilith 1:23-4+ Fall '76.

Friedan at 55. A. Stone. Lilith 1:11-12+ Fall '76.

Marjorie Morningstar revisited. E. Lester. Lilith 1:13-15+ Fall '76.

Sexist cop-out. S. Sugarman. Letter. Response 10:121 Sp '76.

Women on synagogue boards. J.D. Bleich. Trad 15:53-67 Sp '76.

Women's liberation -- an Orthodox response. C.K. Poupko; D.L. Wohlgelernter. Trad 15:45-52 Sp '76.

Will the real pioneers please stand? Editorial. Recon 42:5-6 My '76.

Radical feminism. Letters. S. Brownmiller; D.M. Szony; S.G. Sanders: C.H. Siegel; C. Green. Reply M. Novak. Commentary 61:4+ My '76.

Peace without honor: the battle of the sexes in Israel. N. Stiller. Mid 22:33-41 My '76.

Women's power and status in Jewish communal life: a look at the UJA. S.M. Cohen; S.C. Dessel; M.A. Pelavin. Response 9:59-66 W '75/'76.

The feminine through a (male) glass darkly: preface to a demythology. J. Rosenberg. Response 9:67-88 W '75/'76.

Perception of masculinity among males in two traditional family groups. Nicholas Robak; Sylvia Clavan. Sociological Analysis 1975, 36, 4, Win, 335-346.

Women's liberation -- the second fall of man? Jew Life 41-3 Tishrei 5736 (Fall '75).

Co-eds taking traditional male synagogue roles. S. Spiegler. J Jew Com Ser 52:106-7 Fall '75.

Elements of male chauvinism in classical halakhah. P. Sigal. Jud 24:226-44 Sp '75.

Sexist language. T. Weiss-Rosmarin. Editorial. Jew Spec 40;13-14 Sp '75.

SINGLE-PARENT FAMILIES

The divorced-parent family and the synagogue community. Barbara K. Bundt. Conservative Judaism, Winter 1982.

Developing networks of services to single parents. Estelle Handelman. J Jew Com Ser, Fall 1981.

Services to the child in the single parent family. S. Lerner. J Jew Com Ser 55:369-74 Sum '79.

Family, parent and adult education; Asti; Owings Mill project; A walking tour; Intergenerational Shabbaton; Family Hebrew language learning; Communicating; The Jewish child every day. Ped Rep 28:10-12+ W '77.

The fatherless boys project of the Jewish Board of Guardians: some therapeutic implications. R. Stark. Address. J Jew Com Ser 53:201-7 W '76.

The Jewish community center: a group for adolescents from one-parent families. J. Wolkoff; D. Applebaum. Address. J Jew Com Ser 53:179-84 W '76.

The single parent family. G.B. Bubis. Address. Recon 42:7-10 F '76.

The single-parent family. G.L. Schulman. Address. J Jew Com Ser 51:381-8 Sum '75.

The single parent; a growing challenge to communal service. H. Davis; E. Finkel. Address. J Jew Com Ser 50:251-6 Sp '74.

Helping the single mother through the group process. E. Geggel; R.L. Schwartz. J Jew Com Ser 50:245-56 Sp '74.

SINGLES

Patterns of date and mate selection and social activity of Jewish "singles" in an intermediate community. M.S. Gottlieb; A.C. Heiligman. J Jew Com Ser 58:253-5 Sp '82.

Special issue on non-marital cohabitation. Alternative Life Styles, November 1981.

Singles. M. Farhi. Letter. Jew Spec 45:59 Fall '80.

SINGLES

Are good Jewish men a vanishing breed? W. Novak. cond <u>Jew</u> <u>Digest</u> 25:9-16 Je '80.

Vanishing men - and women? J.D. Cohen. Letter. <u>Moment</u> 5:6-7 Ap '80.

The armchair single. N. Bluestone. <u>Moment,</u> Vol, 5, pp. 37-41 March 1980.

The family in transition; a search for new answers. E. Lauter. <u>Reconstructionist</u> 45, pp. 13-17, January 1980.

To the editor. S. Balter. <u>Con Jud</u> 32:111-12 W '79.

On single rabbihood. R.N. Levine. <u>Response</u> 12:65-7 Sum '79.

New etiquette meets Jewish tradition. M.K. Milton. cond <u>Jew</u> <u>Digest</u> 24:73-6 Je '79.

Socializing, support and Shabbat. C. Neff. <u>Nat Jew Mo</u> 93:20-2 My '79.

Neurotic? R. Weldon. Letter. <u>Nat Jew Mo</u> 95:58 D '78.

The unmarried Jew: problems and prospects. V.A. Zelizer. <u>Con Jud</u> 32:15-21 Fall '78.

Matchmaker, matchmaker, where are you now that we need you? E.A. Solender. cond <u>Jew Digest</u> 22:7-10 Je '77.

Computerized matchmaking. C. Force. <u>Un Syn Rev</u> 29:10-11+ Ap '77.

The life of Jewish singles. N. Bluestone. cond <u>Jew Digest</u> 22:3-9 Ja '77.

Jewish singles. Letter. M. Small. <u>Mid</u> 22:80 Mr '76.

Jewish singles. J.N. Porter. <u>Mid</u> 21:35-43 D '75.

Jewish values in the clinical casework process. P.D. Goldberg. <u>J Jew Com Ser</u> 51:270-9 Sp '75.

Housing problem for the single. J. Carr. <u>Jew Ob</u> 23:19-20 Ap 19 '74.

SINGLES

Young Jews in limbo. P. Dreier. Cong bi-W 40:12-14 O 26 '73.

SURVIVAL, JEWISH

There are compelling reasons to keep the birth-rate up... S. Marcus; R. Bachi. Israel Scene 10-11 Ja '81.

Is American Jewry doomed? T. Weiss-Rosmarin. Editorial. Jew Spec 43:7-11 Sp '78.

Meeting the challenge. L.L. Kaplan. Jew Spec 43:25-8 Sp '78.

How to avoid disappearing. A.A. Cohen. Present Tense 5:64 Sp '78.

Can Judaism survive in isolated suburbs? J.E. Adams. cond Jew Digest 23:29-31 Mr '78.

Planning for the survival of American Jewry. Editorial. Recon 43:5-6 Ja '78.

Living in a Jewish way. A.S. Maller. Jew Spec 42:46-7 Sp '77.

Survival imperatives after the holocaust. R.T. Alpert. Address. Recon 43:7-11 Ap '77.

How Jewry has served America. A.J. Karp. Address. cond Jew Digest 21:77-83 J/Ag '76.

On becoming a Jewish human being. L. Edelman. Nat Jew Mo 90:36+ O '76.

The Jewish family: looking for a usable past. pt 2 P. Hyman. Cong Mo 42:10-11+ O '75.

Crisis and faith. E. Berkovits. Trad 14:5-19 Fall '74.

Jewish survival's secret weapon. C.S. Liebman. Address. cond Jew Digest 19:51-2 Ag '74.

Vanishing American Jewry. H. Goldmeier. Cong bi-W 41:9-11 Je 21 '74.

Jews are an endangered species. A.S. Maller. Amer Zion 65:26-7 S '74.

VALUES AND MORALS

Religion as a factor in morality research: a cross-sectional analysis of older adolescents, young adults, middle-age and senior citizens. C. Stevens; A.M. Blank; G. Poushinsky. J Psychology and Jud 1:61-80 Sp '77.

The implications of moral stages for adult education. L. Kohlberg. Rel Ed 72:183-201 Mr-Ap '77.

Research on adult moral development: Where is it? J.H. Peatling. Rel Ed 72:212-24 Mr-Ap '77.

The ghetto child and moral development. J. Sams. Rel Ed 70:636-48 N/D '75.

Developing Jewish values clarification. S. Rossel. Ped Rep 27:17-21 Fall '75.

Community sanctions, Jewishness and the chillul ha-Shem of nursing home scandal. L.E. Bellin. Address. J Jew Com Ser 52:28-33 Fall '75.

The moral development of children in three different school settings. S. Selig; G. Teller. Rel Ed 70:406-15 Jl/Ag '75.

WOMEN

The shammes is a she. J. Konheim. Con Jud 36;81-3 Fall '82.

A unique feminism. R. Furstenberg. Mid 28:35-9 O '82.

"Baruch Ha'Shem, not so good": some concerns of Jewish women. J. Wolf. Jew Life 6:47-53 Sp/Sum '82.

Towards a feminist theology. L. Cohn-Sherbok. Jew Spec 47:53-5 Sum '82.

An equal or a ward: how independent is a married woman according to Rabbinic law? S. Morrell. Jew SS 44:189-210 Sum/Fall '82.

The role of women in Jewish religious life: a decade of change 1972-1982. Francine Klageburn, et al. AJC Proceedings, June 1982.

Jewish models. W. Abrams. Letter. Moment 7:4-5 Ap '82.

Women (not saying kaddish). C. Kessner. Letter. Moment 7:6 D '81.

WOMEN

Sexuality of deviant females: adolescent and adult correlates. Peter
Paul Vitaliano; Jennifer James; Debra Boyer. Social Work, November
1981.

Kaplan on women in Jewish life. C. Kessner. Recon 47:38-9+ Jl/Ag
'81.

Women in the synagogue today. D.J. Elazar; R.G. Monson. Mid
27:25-30 Ap '81.

Having babies again. N. Munson. Commentary 71:60-3 Ap '81.

Bima. P. Tishman. Lilith No. 8:48 '81.

Survey on women. Lilith No. 8:9 '81.

Feminists against anti-semitism. Lilith No. 8:10 '81.

Working daughters. S.S. Weinberg. Lilith No. 8:20-3 '81.

The American Orthodox Jewish housewife. Blanche Frank. Contemporary Jewry, Fall/Winter 1980.

Women as wives in Jewish tradition; Husband's duties; Bad wives and
good wives. ADL Bull 37:7 O '80.

Three generations of women today. G.H. Kremer. cond Jew Digest
26;6-11 O '80.

Social justice and women's rights in Jewish tradition. F. Klagsbrun.
ADL Bul 37:5-6+ O '80.

Women on their own. BEW enters the 1980s. B. Joselow. Nat Jew
Mo 95:58-63 Ag-S '80.

Some observations on the role of American Jewish women as
communal volunteers. il J. Sochen. Amer Jew Hist 70:23-34 S '80.

Torah-true and feminist too: a psychotherapist's view of the conflict
of Orthodox Judaism and the women's movement. A. Clamar.
Address. J Jew Com Ser 56:297-300 Sum '80.

Women of yesterday. E.D. Freud. Letter. Jew Spec 45:60 Sp '80.

Jewish women face the eighties. S.W. Schneider. Keeping Posted
25:3-7 F '80.

WOMEN

How to get what we want by the year 2000. E.S. Elwell; R.G. Monson; A.G Wolfe; A. Daum; R.T. Alpert; I. Fine; J. Litman; E.M. Broner. Lilith No. 7:18-22 '80.

"Study" Orthodox women told. M. Chernick. Lilith No. 7:42 '80.

Women against women. T. Weiss-Rosmarin. Editorial. Jew Spec 44:8-9 W '79.

The Jewish attitude towards women. J.B. Segal. J Jew Stud 30:121-37 Autumn '79.

From patriarchy to partnership - the evolution of the Jewish woman. J. Rosenberg. J Jew Com Ser 55:339-44 Sum '79.

Deification and disdain: a literary view of black and Jewish mothers. M. Zak. J Psychology and Jud 3:268-77 Sum '79.

Sex according to the Song of Songs. H. Maccoby. Commentary 67:53-9 Je '79.

Women's role - some ultimate concerns. R.P. Bulka. Trad 17:27-40 Sp '79.

Observations: what women want. B. Berger. Commentary 67:62-6 Mr '79.

The women's role: a continuing discussion. M. Shapiro. Con Jud 32:63-6 Fall '78.

The women's role. C.H. Pearl. Con Jud 32:67-70 Fall '78.

Women, education and industrialization: a comparative analysis of Jewish, Ghanaian and Vietnamese women. Lois Weis; and others. Oct 1978, 26p. Paper presented at the Comparative Social Development State of the Art Conference (Columbia, MO, October 29-30, 1978).

Jewish feminism on the move. B. Greenberg. ADL Bull 35:4-5 S '78.

May women be taught Bible, Mishnah and Talmud? A.M. Silver. Trad 17:74-85 Sum '78.

The myth of the Jewish mother in three Jewish, American, female writers. Jacqueline A. Mintz. Centennial Review 1978, 22, 3, Summer, 346-355.

WOMEN

What's a Jewish mother. Children's essays. Lilith 1:18-20 F/W '77/'78.

The historical national women's conference in Houston. Jewish organizations pledge support. H.S. Lewis. Jew Fron 45:13-15+ Ja '78.

Jewish businesswomen in America. I.D. Neu. cond Jew Digest 23:39-48 D '77.

Letters. I.C. Selavan. Moment 3:3 N '77.

Is feminism good for the Jews? A.C. Zuckoff. cond Jew Digest 23:60-2 O '77.

The "real" Jewish mother? R. Adler. Mid 23:38-40 O '77.

Italian, Jewish, and Slavic grandmothers in Pittsburgh: their economic roles. Corinne Azen Krause. Frontiers 1977, 2, 2, Summer, 18-28.

Jewish women: coming of age. B. Greenberg. Trad 16:79-94 Sum '77.

Where are the women? more and more doing the same jobs as men. E. Solender. il Moment 2:33-6+ Je '77.

How the Jewish feminist movement was born. A.L. Lerner. cond Jew Digest 22:35-8 My '77.

With "woman" in the title. G.S. Rotenberg. Jew Spec 41:29-31 W '76.

The Jewish business woman in America. I.D. New. Amer Jew Hist Q 66:137-54 S '76.

Letters on B. Greenberg's article. H.G. Borgenicht; A.E. Elman; E. Gerstle; G. Green; G. Hod; H. Weiner. Had Mag 57:22 Me '76.

Feminism. P. Kornspan. Letter. Had Mag 57:22 Je '76.

Blu Greenberg replies. Letter. Had Mag 57:24 Je '76.

Feminism - is it good for the Jews? B. Greenberg. Excerpt adapt The Jewish woman: new perspectives. ed Elizabeth Koltun. Had Mag 57:10-11+ Ap '76.

WOMEN

Haven't you got enough to do at home? J. Rose. Present Tense 2:6-8 W '75.

Jewish daughters of the revolution. B. Postal. cond Jew Digest 21:30-3 D '75.

Jewish feminism: some second thoughts. N. Fuchs-Kreimer. cond Jew Digest 21:8-11 D '75.

Tradition! Tradition! S. Spiegler. J Jew Com Ser 52:217 W '75.

Today's Jewish woman: the challenge of change. Address. V.S. Margolis. J Jew Com Ser 52:145-52 W '75.

In the door of the tent. R.G. Strauss. il. Un Syn R 28:12-13+ Fall '75.

Jewish women. M. Ackelsberg. Letter. Moment 1;8-10 Jl/Ag '75.

Feminists for Judaism. S.F. Segal. Mid 21:59-65 Ag/S '75.

Feminism and Judaism. L. Pfeffer. Cong Mo 42:12-14 Je '75.

Time for women to come forward. J. Kahanoff. Reprint. Jew Ob 24:10-11 My 16 '75.

Changing stereotype of Jewish women in the popular culture. Judith Frankel; Norman Mirsky. 1975, 10p. Paper presented at the national Convention of The Popular Culture Association (5th, St. Louis, March 20-22, 1975).

Sarah's seed. A new ritual for women. M. Gendler. Response No 24:65-75 W '74/'75.

Cancer risks in Jewish women. R. Kushner. Nat Jew Mo 89:36-9 D '74.

Women and success. S. Rudikoff. Commentary 58:49-59 O '74.

The Jewish woman and her heritage. S. Singer. Recon 40;10-17 O '74.

A new consciousness among Jewish women. E. Faust-Levy. Amer Zion 64:27-32 Je '74.

WOMEN

Women and Jewish studies. E.R. Levenson. Letter. Jew Spec 39:69 Sum '74.

Our own equal rights movement. S. Spiegler. J Jew Com Ser 50:372-3 Sum '74.

To the editor! "The Jewish women." J. Hollander. Response 21:21-2 Sp '74.

Women in American Jewish life. D.J. Elazar. Cong bi-W 40:10-11 N 23 '73.

Women in Conservative synagogues. T. Weiss-Rosmarin. Jew Spec 38:5-6 O '73.

Women write about women. S. Schneider. Had Mag 55:21-2 O '73.

Naming the girl. P. Swerdlow. Letter. Jew Spec 38:27-8 S '73.

Female consciousnes-raising. T. Weiss-Rosmarin. Editorial. Jew Spec 38:4-6+ S '73.

Families that stay together...pray together? E. Gertel. Un Syn Rev 26:12-13+ Fall '73.

The female of the species. ADL Bull 30:7-8 F '73.

The changing role of women in the Jewish community. pt. 1. J.K. Levine. Address. Cong bi-W 40:8-11 F 23 '73.

Do ten Ms's make a minyan? S. Spiegler. J Jew Com Ser 50:104 Fall '73.

Negativism and feminism. M. Spero. Jew Life 40:22-5 Jl '73.

The Jewish woman: an anthology. Elizabeth Kolton, editor. Response, No. 18, Summer 1973.

The other half: women in the Jewish tradition. P.E. Hyman. Response 18:67-75 Sum '73.

The changing role of women in the Jewish community. J.K. Levine. Address. Response 18:59-65 Sum '73.

The Jew who wasn't there: halacha and the Jewish woman. R. Adler. Response 18:77-89 Sum '73.

WOMEN

The Jewish feminist: conflict in identities.   J.P. Goldenberg. Address.
Response 18:11-18 Sum '73.

The Jewish woman in the responsa (900 C.E.-1500 C.E.)   I. Epstein.
Response 18:23-31 Sum '73.

One woman's religious concerns within heterodoxy.   K.   Green.
Response 19:19-21 Sum '73.

The oppression of the Jewish woman.   A.C. Zuckoff.   Response
18;47-54 Sum '73.

A selected bibliography.   Response 18:183-7 Sum '73.

Changing role of women in the Jewish community.   J. Levine.
Congress bi-W, February 1973.

Money, the job, and little women.   E. Moers.   Excerpt. Commentary
55:57-65 Ja '73.

WOMEN AS RABBIS

The woman rabbi: an historical perspective.   A. Guttmann.   J Reform
Jud 29:21-5 Sum '82.

Women in the rabbinate: a moment of real change.   R.S.   Friedman.
Jew Fron 49:12-16+ Ja '82.

Women rabbis.   S.S. Romain.   European Jud 15:31-2 W '81.

Women and Judaism.   J. Neuberger.   European Jud 15:29 W '81.

Report on women in the rabbinate.   B. Borts.   European Jud 15:30-1
W '81.

Whither women rabbis?   K.L. Fox.   Rel Ed 76:361-8 Jl-Ag '81.

Women as rabbis.   Reply to letter.   R. Gordis.   Mid 27:62-4 Ap '81.

Women and the rabbinate.   Letters.   N.A. Barack; H.M. Schulweis;
W.S. Wurzburger; B. Levine; D. Novak.   Mid 27:60-2 Ap '81.

Mazel tov: women ordained as rabbis 1981.   Women cantors. Lilith No
8:36 '81.

WOMEN AS RABBIS

Conservative rabbis endorse women's ordination. R.S. Friedman. Lilith No 7:6-7 '80.

On our minds. Response No 38:4-5 '80.

Women and the rabbinate. R.S. Friedman. Keeping Posted 26:13-14 D '80.

On being a woman rabbi. S. Levine. Keeping Posted 25:22-3 F '80.

Israeli women and the rabbinate. Y. Har-Shefi. Interview. Keeping Posted 25:20-2 F '80.

The ordination of women. R. Gordis. Mid 26:25-32 Ag-S '80.

Women rabbis. J.S. Pila. Letter. Moment 5:3+ Jl-Ag '80.

First Jewish woman chaplain. (United States Army) S. Spiegler. J Jew Com Ser 56:282 Sp '80.

The Conservative condition. D. Szonyi. Moment 5:38-42 My '80.

Our readers speak: women as rabbis. Moment 5:34-7 My '80.

Women as rabbis. M.R. Rudin. Present Tense 6:44-8 W '79.

The politics of women's ordination. R.S. Friedman. Lilith No 6:9-15 '79.

Is it good for the Conservative movement? Editorial. Recon 45:5-6 D '79.

Women as Conservative rabbis? R.R. Wisse. Commentary 68:59-64 O '79.

Women as rabbis: a partisan view. M.M. Fenster. Cong Mo 46:11-13 S-O '79.

On the ordination of women. E.A. Wernick. Jew Spec 44:57-8 Fall '79.

Female rabbis. G. Tucker. Letter. Jew Spec 44:59-60 Fall '79.

Women as Conservative rabbis. I.H. Levinthal. Letter. Jew Spec 44:59-60 Sum '79.

WOMEN AS RABBIS

Woman rabbi. M. Bernstein. Letter. Reply M.R. Rudin. Present Tense 6:3-4 Sum '79.

On the ordination of women. G.D. Cohen. Cond Jud 32:56-62 Sum '79.

Final report of the Commission for the study of the ordination of women as rabbis. Con Jud 32:63-80 Sum '79.

Not a woman rabbi or a lady rabbi but a rabbi. C. Yalkut. Nat Jew Mo 93:6-8+ Mr '79.

Will the conservative movement move? Editorial. Recon 45:3-5 Mr '79.

Final report of the Commission for the study of the ordination of women as rabbis. Jew Spec 44:48-56 Sp '79.

Letter to the editor. E. Borowitz. Lilith 1:3-4 F/W '77/'78.

Preisand (sic) and prejudice. Letters. J.L. Kessler; J. Schulman. Moment 3:4+ S '78.

Women and Reform Judaism. Keeping Posted 24:19-20 S '78.

Rabbi Sally. R. Mecklenburger. Letter. Moment 3:4 Jl-Ag '78.

Conservative women rabbis? Editorial. Recon 43:4-5 D '77.

Gentlemen's agreement at the Seminary. A. Stone. Lilith 1:13-18 Sp/Sum '77.

Women as conservative rabbis. Our readers respond. (Letters) Un Syn Rev 29:16-17+ Ap '77.

My daughter the rabbi. M.E. Thornton. Jew Digest 22:3-6 O '76.

Why not women as Conservative rabbis? J. Ofseyer. Un Syn Rev 29:6-7+ Fall '76.

Women's liberation and Jewish law. B. Greenberg. Lilith 1:16-19+ Fall '76.

Sight and sound; Cultural conference; Russian phenomenon; Voices of women; Follow-up. H.G. Goodman. Had Mag 57:39-40 Mr '76.

WOMEN AS RABBIS

Of women rabbis and halakhah. Editorial. Recon 40:5-6 Je '74.

The rabbis in new roles. Recon 40:5-6 My '74.

Woman in the pulpit. E. Starkman. Had Mag 56:15+ D '73.

YOUTH

Sixties youth, Zionist youth. D. Frazer. Forum No 44:25-36 Sp '82.

Meeting the challenge of contemporary youth. L.R. Wunsch. Ped Forum in Ped Rep 33:32-4 Mr '82.

Connecting the unconnected; reaching out to high school youth. J Katz. Address. J Jew Com Ser 58:42-6 Fall '81.

Child adults. S. Levin. Mid 27:41-6 O '81.

Youth: chance of a lifetime. G. Sifrin. Israel Scene 32-4 O '81.

Youth: banding together. G. Vromen. Israel Scene 23-4 Jl '81.

Identity status of Jewish youth: pre- and post-cultural involvement. Idy Gitelson and Edward Reed. J Jew Com Ser, Summer 1981.

High school: coping as a Jewish teen; Jewish youth coalition; Integrated teen program (academic and informal); College credit courses for high schoolers. Ped Rep 32:9-10 Ap '81.

The giants of Jerusalem. What happens to the perceptions of American teenagers when they encounter old people in a Jerusalem courtyard? D. Siegel. Moment 6:44-7 Mr-Ap '81.

Close encounters. D. Geffen. Israel Scene 14 Mr '81.

Special issue youth and anti-semitism. ADL Youth Bull 38: F '81.

Call to Jewish youth: 1901 symposium: the future of the Labor Zionist idea. N. Syrkin. Jew Fron 48:20-3 Ja '81.

A black-Jewish success story. (Northwestern High School, Baltimore, Maryland) J. Goldberg. cond Jew Digest 25:26-31 Je '80.

Modern problems of Jewish parents. J. Kohn. Excerpts. Recon 45:18-21 Ja '80.

YOUTH

Bar Mitzvah: a rite for a transitional age. Susan Zegans; Leonard S. Zegans. Psychoanalytic Review 1979, 66, 1, Spring, 115-132.

Alternative lifestyles in the U.S.; a presentation 14th American Israel dialogue. M. Decter. Cong Mo 46:27-9 F/Mr '79.

This is a defeat for Jewish students. E. Freedman. Response 11:19-24 Sum '78.

Project: student lay advocacy on behalf of aged persons. J. Maman; J.D. Schwartz. J Jew Com Ser 54:321-4 Sum '78.

Self, family, and community: a cross-cultural comparison of American and Israeli youth. Tamar Becker. Youth and Society 1976, 8, 1, Sep, 45-66.

Unity for youth. Jew Ob 25:3 Je 25 '76.

Youth movements feel left out. Z. Lewis. Jew Ob 25:11 F 6 '76.

Why youth is not mobilized. Jew Ob 25:18 Ja 9 '76.

Religion and the expectations of modern society towards the adolescent. I. Knox. Rel Ed 70:349-60 N/D '75.

Unfortunate exodus. Jew Ob 24:2 N 21 '75.

Pride and discipline in the Jewish Poconos. H. Epstein. Nat Jew Mo 90:28+ O '75.

Controversy: challenges for the younger generation. S. Levenberg. Jew Ob 24:15 Ag 8 '75.

Consider the frummie and the in-betweenie, but beware of the chnyoyk. D. Siegel. Nat Jew Mo 89:42-4+ Jl/Ag '75.

A pad for Torah rapping. E. Starkman. cond Jew Digest 20:21-5 Ap '75.

Staying power. Jew Ob 24:3 Ap 4 '75.

Time for action among youth movements. Letter. S. Forman. Jew Ob 24:11 Ap 4 '75.

A youth aliyah success story. R. Seligman. Had Mag 56:16+ D '74.

YOUTH

A challenge to youth. Jew Ob 23:3 S 27 '74.

Turning onto Torah. D. Fruchter. Jew Life 41:11-17 Sum '74.

Reaching out to adolescents: foundation and form. S. Donshik. Address. J Jew Com Ser 50:349-58 Sum '74.

Jewish teenagers are different. A.S. Maller. cond Jew Digest 19:19-22 Ag '74.

Religious pluralism, political values and American teenagers. A.S. Maller. Rel Ed 69:446-50 Jl/Ag '74.

Student activity "needs reorganizing." Jew Ob 23:29 Mr 29 '74.

Bring young Jews back to the synagogue. M.A. Yoskowitz. Con Jud 28:77-9 Sp '74.

NFTY's national academy; to enrich our life. S.M. Sandmel. CCARJ 21:26-8 Sp '74.

"Come and help us now"; Israel's call to diaspora youth. Jew Ob 23:24 Ja 11 '74.

The occult and the Jewish community. S. Siegel. cond Jew Digest 19:19-23 n '73.

Against misinformation. J. Aumente. Jew Ob 30;7-8 O '73.

Two arrivals. E. Zuroff. Jew Life 41:22-7 O '73.

The conflicts of Jewish youth. R. Kronish. Cong bi-W 40:10-12 Je 15 '73.

The youth: Jews, Israelis, or both? S.N. Herman. Jud 22:167-72 Sp '73.

The youth scene. G. Freidlin. Had Mag 54:46+ My '73.

Where is the challenge? Jew Ob 22:3 Mr 16 '73.

The counter-culture. W.J. Mcgill. ADL Bull 30:4-5 Ja '73.

Youth shows the way. Jew Ob 22:3 Ja 5 '73.

ABBREVIATIONS

ADL Bull - Anti-Defamation League Bulletin
Amer Jew Arc - American Jewish Archives
Amer Jew Hist Q - American Jewish Historical Quarterly
Amer Zion - American Zionist
CCARJ - Central Conference of American Rabbis Journal
Con Jud - Conservative Judaism
Cong bi-W - Congaress Bi-Weekly
Cong Mo - Congress Monthly
European Jud - European Judaism
Had Mag - Hadassah Magazine
J American Demographics - Journal of American Demographics
J Bib Lit - Journal of Biblical Literature
J Jew Com Ser - Journal of Jewish Communal Service
J Jew Stud - Journal of Jewish Studies
J Psychology and Jud - Journal of Psychology and Judaism
J Reform Jud - Journal of Reform Judaism
Jerusalem Q - Jerusalem Quarterly
Jew Digest - Jewish Digest
Jew Ed - Jewish Education
Jew Fron - Jewish Frontier
Jew Heritage - Jewish Heritage
Jew J Soc - Jewish Journal of Sociology
Jew Life - Jewish Life
Jew Ob - Jewish Observer
Jew Q R - Jewish Quarterly Review
Jew Spec - Jewish Spectator
Jew SS - Jewish Social Studies
Jud - Judaism
Mid - Midstream
Nat Jew Mo - National Jewish Monthly
NCJW - National Council of Jewish Women
Pat Prej - Patterns of Prejudice
Ped Rep - Pedagogic Reporter
Recon - Reconstructionist
Rel Ed - Religious Education
Syn Sch - Synagogue School
Trad - Tradition
Un Syn Rev - United Synagogue Review
West States Jew Hist Q - Western States Jewish Historical Quarterly

ABOUT THE AUTHOR

Gerald B. Bubis is the founding Director of the School of Jewish Communal Service at Hebrew Union College - Jewish Institute of Religion, Los Angeles Campus. He has served there since July, 1968 where he is also the Alfred Gottschalk Professor of Jewish Communal Studies. He serves as Vice President of the Jerusalem Center for Public Affairs.

He has coauthored, authored and/or edited five books and monographs and over sixty articles relating to aspects of Contemporary Jewish life.

In addition to lecturing and serving as a consultant and conducting services throughout North America, Europe and Israel, he serves on many local, national and international boards of directors which are devoted to Jewish communal and/or family life.

As a social worker prior to joining Hebrew Union College - Jewish Institute of Religion, Professor Bubis held a number of administrative posts in Hillel, camping, Jewish community center and Jewish federations.